12-3-96

Thought Contagion

Thought Contagion

How Belief Spreads Through Society

AARON LYNCH

BasicBooks
A Division of HarperCollins*Publishers*

FIRST EDITION

Designed by Nancy Sabato

Library of Congress Cataloging-in-Publication Data

Lynch, Aaron.
    Thought contagion : how belief spreads through society / Aaron Lynch. —
1st ed.
        p.   cm.
    Includes bibliographical references and index.
    ISBN 0-465-08466-4
    1. Social psychology.   2. Contagion (Social psychology).   I. Title.
HM251.L95   1996
302—dc20   96-41489

96 97 98 99 00 ❖/HC 10 9 8 7 6 5 4 3 2 1

To
Carl and Flo

CONTENTS

ACKNOWLEDGMENTS

I am grateful to numerous people who have helped me develop this book and the theory behind it. For the extraordinary generosity that made this work possible, I owe my gratitude to Carl Wegner. Douglas R. Hofstadter helped immensely through his encouragement, thought-provoking correspondence, and access to a fine publishing house. Special thanks to Curt Hicks and Michael J. Crowley for making long and inspired contributions to content and prose.

For valuable improvements in the months before publication, I thank Richard Fumosa and Chris Korintus of Basic Books. For helping me with earlier drafts, I thank Manor Askenazi, Alan Baumbaugh, David Eisenman, Janice Feldstein, Karen Green, Michael Goldhaber, Karen Heffernan, Karen Howarth, Dee Hull, and Virginia McCullough.

I also thank the many people at Fermilab and the University of Illinois who gave both encouragement and constructive criticism.

1

SELF-SENT MESSAGES AND MASS BELIEF

Man is what he believes.
—ANTON CHEKHOV

A religious taboo against modern farm machines is growing more widespread among American farmers, and for an unusual reason. The taboo, held by Old Order Amish farmers, keeps increasing because it creates a need for manual labor. Amish farmers meet this need by raising many children, who start farm work very young. Consequently, these farmers pass their taboo down to a large number of children: many children, ergo many young taboo-holders. As documented in John Hostetler's *Amish Society,* their population doubles in just twenty-three years—much faster than the American or even world population doubles. With each generation, the Amish ideas rule a larger percentage of American farmers' lives. (See figure 1.)

FIGURE 1

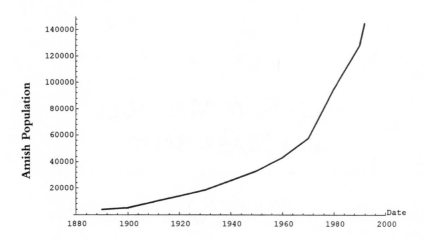

Amish Belief Propagation. Old ways boom in modern times: Graph shows the explosive growth of the Old Order Amish during the past century, rising forty-fold as a result of very high birthrates. *Source:* John Hostetler, Amish Society (Baltimore: Johns Hopkins University Press), 4th ed., pp. 97–98.

THE SELF-PROPAGATING IDEA

The Amish farming taboo is a self-propagating idea, or *thought contagion*. Though that taboo has not yet become a widespread norm, many self-propagating ideas achieved that level of success decades, generations, even centuries ago. Overlooked by established social sciences, thought contagion warrants more attention as a force shaping society.

Like a software virus in a computer network or a physical virus in a city, thought contagions proliferate by effectively "programming" for their own retransmission. Beliefs affect retransmission in so many ways that they set off a colorful, unplanned growth race among diverse "epidemics" of ideas. Actively contagious ideas are now called *memes* (a word that rhymes with "teams") by students of the newly emerging science of *memetics*.

Though the analogy between cultural and biological contagion was recognized at least by the 1950s, the evolutionary biologist Richard Dawkins expressed it at full strength in the last chapter of his 1976 book, *The Selfish Gene*. This short chapter, in which Dawkins coins the word *meme,* launched a slowly smoldering first twenty years of memetics. Those decades also saw comparable contributions by Douglas Hofstadter and Daniel Dennett, among others.

The present book aims to expand memetics far beyond an academic curiosity by examining its vast relevance to how society thinks and lives. A treatment of this new field can presently offer just an outline, a thumbnail sketch of a far-reaching science. Yet seeing the new paradigm linked with so many important aspects of life imparts a revised worldview, one that renders apparently arbitrary currents of culture freshly comprehensible.

MODES OF THOUGHT CONTAGION

The ways that memes retransmit fit into seven general patterns called *modes:* the quantity parental, efficiency parental, proselytic, preservational, adversative, cognitive, and motivational modes. Each one involves a thought contagion's "carrier," or *host,* serving to increase the idea's "infected" group, or *host population*.

THE QUANTITY OF PARENTHOOD

Any idea influencing its hosts to have more children than they would otherwise have exhibits *quantity parental* transmission. Because of children's special receptivity to parental ideas, increasing the number of children increases the projected number of host offspring. So the Amish farming taboo has a quantity parental advantage.

Far more prevalent in North America is the taboo against

masturbation. Its vast influence shows up clearly in the recent "Sex in America Survey," and vividly in events that brought down a recent surgeon general.

The Census Bureau does not track fertility rates for this taboo's hosts, so its quantity parental effect is less demonstrable than that of the Amish faith. Yet educated guesswork suggests that the masturbation taboo raises its adherents' reproduction rate above average levels. Taboo hosts generally have fewer acceptable options for reacting to sex drives. They must either mate more often, abstain more often, or do both. The resulting behavioral mix should contribute more children to the taboo's host population. Even hosts whose masturbation remains unabated would still experience guilt as a motive to seek entirely partnered sex. This group's greater effort toward mating would presumably yield more children to inculcate with the taboo.

The number of extra children per generation need not be great to explain the masturbation taboo's widespread propagation. The secret lies in the taboo's very great age. Even a 5 percent per generation increase amounts to a 132-fold increase when compounded over 100 generations. A reproductive effect imperceptible to any one generation can gently elevate the idea from fringe group status to mainstream proportions. Such modern influences as publicized sex research have reversed some of the taboo's gains, though the subject of masturbation still troubles many.

THE EFFICIENCY OF PARENTHOOD

Simply having children cannot guarantee that any will embrace the parents' beliefs. Yet some beliefs actually stack their odds of acceptance by guiding the methods of parenthood. Any idea increasing the fraction of its hosts' children who eventually adopt their parents' meme exhibits *efficiency parental* transmission.

To illustrate, Amish carry a belief that Amish must stay

highly separated from non-Amish. This separatism saturates Amish children with Amish ideas (including separatism) while "protecting" them from non-Amish memes. So Amish separatists impart their faith to offspring more successfully than do nonseparatist Amish. This keeps the majority of Amish abidingly separatist. By staying segregated, the Amish get 78 percent of their children to stick with the faith in a predominantly non-Amish country. The same transmission efficiency gained by Amish separatism may also intensify other separatist movements around the world.

The evolutionary biologists Eytan Avital and Eva Jablonka in Israel recently coined the name *phenotypic cloning* to describe such parentally replicated memes in humans and other animals. Their work focuses mainly on basic skills, but the concept applies equally to everything from ingrained personalities to conscious beliefs.

PROSELYTIZING PAYS

Thought contagions spread fastest via *proselytic* transmission. A proselytic idea's hosts generally pass the idea to people other than just their own children. Such propagation is not slowed by the years needed to raise children. Host populations seldom double *parentally* every ten years, but a proselytically spreading idea, under suitable conditions, can double its host population in a year or less.

The conviction "My country is dangerously low on weapons" illustrates proselytic advantage. The idea strikes fear in its hosts for both their own and their compatriots' lives. That fear drives them to persuade others of military weakness to build pressure for doing something about it. So the belief, through the side effect of fear, triggers proselytizing. Meanwhile, alternative opinions such as "My country has enough weaponry" promote a sense of security and less urgency about changing others' minds. Thus, belief in a weapons shortage can self-propagate to majority proportions— even in a country of unmatched strength. In the United States, the meme spread widely during the late 1970s and early 1980s despite a great superiority in military hardware. Though the impressive buildup that followed may have helped end the cold war, the prerequisite opinion shift came from thought contagions spreading in people who expected a permanent cold war.

Proselytic thought contagion becomes self-limiting as host population growth diminishes the supply of nonhosts. Few nonhosts remain by the time the host population is a great majority since most have already converted by then. Without enough nonhosts, especially persuadable ones, the proselytizing cannot win many new adherents. This creates cycles in which successful proselytic movements lose momentum, setting the stage for renewed outbreaks of old movements and initial outbreaks of new movements.

PRESERVING BELIEF

In the *preservational mode,* ideas influence their hosts to remain hosts for a long time. The idea may influence its adherents to live longer, or make them avoid dropping out.

A belief that "One should never argue religion or politics" illustrates the dropout-prevention form. The belief substantially immunizes its hosts against religious or political proselytism. This reduces their chances of conversion to any persuasion that emphasizes proselytism—a persuasion that one *should* argue religion or politics. Thus, the argument-avoiding belief preserves its *own* existence among adherents.

The belief may achieve majority status in people who remain unconverted by proselytic religion and politics, leaving proselytic movements to solicit an increasingly "resistant strain" of nonhosts.

SABOTAGING THE COMPETITION

If every proselytic movement spawns a stubborn resistance, the memetic contests would all grind down to stalemates. Yet often they don't. When proselytic zealots become stymied, the only memetic variants that continue to spread are those that carry the movement to a more aggressive phase.

In the *adversative* mode, ideas influence their hosts to attack or sabotage competing movements. That is, the host can either harm nonhost individuals or destroy their memes' ability to spread.

Both mechanisms occur with the Muslim belief—supported by the Koran—that God rewards those who fight and kill for Islam. First, this idea programs some hosts to selectively kill those who refuse to convert to Islam. Provided that this meme does not lose too many of its own people in the process, the killing increases the *relative* size of its Islamic host population. Second, adherents frighten many surviving non-Muslims into silence, largely destroying their idea's proselytic contagiousness. This, too, reduces the projected number of nonhosts, increasing the relative prevalence of Islam.

Adversative replication advantage occurs only when aggressive action results from the memes themselves, since only then can it favor one movement over another. Other antagonisms, such as those over resources, can happen just as well between like-minded believers—and do not generally work as memetic advantages.

COGNITIVE ADVANTAGE

If an idea seems well founded to most people exposed to it, then nonhosts tend to adopt it, and hosts tend to retain it. That perceived cogency to the total population provides an idea with its *cognitive* advantage.

Of course, what is widely perceived as cogent frequently differs from the truth. When Benjamin Franklin introduced the lightning rod, his idea seemed blasphemous to many clerics thundering from pulpits and presses—all because the populace still saw lightning as punishment from God. Whether an idea seems cogent to specific people depends upon matters ranging from what other ideas they already have to the neurobiological characteristics of humans in general.

One cognitively propagated idea is the belief that "The earth revolves around the sun." Its seeming consistency with many astronomers' observations of the sun at various times of the year made it popular among astronomers. The astronomers, regarded as honest and knowledgeable, then presented their theory to many others clearly and logically. Through its intellectual appeal, the idea gradually expanded its following from the intelligentsia of Copernicus's time to the schoolchildren of today.

Cognitively favored ideas usually spread more passively than ideas emphasizing the other modes. Rather than actively programming the host's retransmitting behavior, the belief's contagiousness depends heavily on the other ideas and cognitive traits of the population. Thus the cognitively propagated idea "is propagated" rather than "propagates itself."

Cognitive advantage plays a strong part in the efficiency parental, proselytic, and preservational modes. After all, perceived cogency largely determines whether a person will adopt an idea on hearing it and retain the idea after adopting it.

MOTIVATIONAL ADVANTAGE

Ideas can also passively amass their host populations through the *motivational mode*. In this mode, people adopt or retain an idea because they have some motive for doing so: that is, because they expect to be better off as hosts than as nonhosts.

The larger the number of people who want to hold a specific idea, and the more strongly they want it, the greater will be its motivational advantage.

Tax revolts illustrate motivational propagation. Many tax-payers hearing the tax revolt meme feel economically motivated to adopt it, accounting for much of its spread. Adherents also feel economically motivated to pass along the idea once they have it, adding proselytism to the movement. Some people, ranging from rich to poor, even express tax revolt memes to give impressions of an affluence that shoulders taxes as its major expense. Still, the obvious motivational appeal of tax revolt ideas accounts for much of their prevalence, even though other factors contribute.

In the motivational mode, as in the cognitive, ideas do not *self*-propagate in a strong sense. Yet motivational propagation plays a frequent supporting role in the efficiency parental, proselytic, and preservational modes.

THE EPIDEMIOLOGY OF IDEAS

Different modes of thought contagion usually occur together. Thus, a single idea has a *propagative profile* consisting of any advantages it has in each mode.

Memetic theory analyzes these propagative profiles in a manner resembling that used in epidemiology. An epidemiologist might conclude, for instance, that sneezing out virus particles accounts for much of the common cold's propagation; the virus's way of causing sneeze-triggering nasal irritation is what makes the cold so common. Similarly, a memeticist might determine that the weapons-shortage belief spreads largely by proselytism; the idea's way of producing proselytism–motivating fear is what makes the belief so common. Memetics is, in part, an *epidemiology* of ideas.

Memetic folkways need not correspond to viral diseases,

and so do not always deserve the same bad reputation. The belief that we should love our neighbors illustrates the benign nature of many thought contagions. The terms *thought contagion* and *epidemiology* therefore carry neutral connotations in the context of memetics theory.

FORMING NEW IDEAS

Thought contagions have an impact on thought creation as new ideas that seem spontaneously created often derive from preexisting ideas. Frequently, this happens by either altering, building upon, or fusing earlier notions. Yet usually much more than just having a precursor belief is necessary for a person to generate a new idea. Any *one* adherent of the earlier idea may be quite unlikely to form the new idea. But as the precursor spreads, the odds increase that someone will make that creative leap. Thought contagions therefore shape creative output at the population level.

As an example, the Mormon faith arose only after the widespread proliferation of the Christian faith. The distinctive Mormon tenet that Jesus of Nazareth visited North America explains the connection: because millions already believed that a true Christ had visited the Middle East, it was far more likely that someone would create the idea that he also visited North America. Very few individuals, Christian or not, create highly original beliefs like this one. Yet Christianity makes good potential starting material. So the more Christians, the greater the likelihood that someone somewhere will create the new variation. This means that all the contagious advantages of Christianity play a powerful role in setting worldwide formation rates for new, but related, ideas—including such Mormon ideas as the belief that Christ visited North America.

RECOMBINING IDEAS

Thought contagion also reshuffles old ideas into novel combinations. Sometimes the recombined beliefs hold new implications that spark completely new ideas. Other times, newly combined beliefs become novel thought contagions in their own right.

Recombination affects, for example, the belief in an imminent and inevitable doomsday. The doomsday idea alone probably does not inspire much proselytism; it may even inspire decisions to let others remain blissfully ignorant of their impending fate.

Now consider the religious belief that whoever dies an unbeliever goes to hell. The hell belief *alone* motivates hosts to convert friends and loved ones. It stirs enough proselytic urgency to spread itself far and wide in the population—far and wide enough that with near certainty it spreads to someone who holds or adopts the doomsday belief. So the hell idea's contagiousness may get most of the credit for generating the first "hell–doomsday" combination.

The two ideas *paired* inspire more proselytic drive than they could separately. After all, an imminent doomsday leaves very little time to save unbelieving friends from hell. The combination's souped-up proselytic drive has greatly enriched the concentration of doomsayers among Christians who believe in hell.

Far-spreading beliefs meet up with each other more often, biasing new combinations to selectively include the most vigorous of what went before. If the beliefs are mutually compatible as combined, the combination spreads even faster as a package. The fast-spreading package, in turn, meets up even faster with other spreading memes. This helps build elaborate bundles of memes that foster their own and each other's propagation.

Population memetics, the study of how proliferating

memes combine and separate in a population, roughly parallels the study of how proliferating genes combine and separate, the branch of biology called population genetics. Indeed, the similarities inspired the evolutionary biologist Richard Dawkins to coin the word *meme* to vaguely resemble the word *gene*.

Yet the realm of ideas, or *ideosphere,* often departs from its analogy to the biosphere. For example, individual occurrences of *genes* "drop out" of the biosphere almost exclusively by "host" organism death. But an *idea's* occurrences may drop out either because hosts die or because hosts convert to nonhosts. This gives the evolution of memes a more complicated mathematical form than the evolution of genes.

MEMETIC EVOLUTION

Meme propagation drives memetic innovation by helping generate and recombine ideas. The beliefs spreading most vigorously prevail in the natural selection of memes, giving them the best odds of spawning new variants and combinations. Such innovation, in turn, drives propagation by supplying both new and strengthened thought contagions. Meme propagation and innovation thus accomplish the great feedback algorithm of Darwinian evolution in the ideosphere. Much as biological evolution keeps viruses renewed and infectious, so too does memetic evolution keep certain beliefs current and contagious. It all happens without plan, and it gives evolving thought contagions a profound influence on society.

A WORLD OF BARRIERS

To some, it can seem naïve, even stupid, to find significance in people's benign resharing of beliefs. In anyone's day-to-day and year-to-year experience, the competition between people usually matters more than the competition between beliefs. A palpable competition between important players also settles much of the month to month business of nations. Rivals often hesitate to share their ideas, and react with distrust when others do; and power plays typically call for withholding information, or imparting outright disinformation. Considering the enormous range of competitive social and economic situations, meme replication would seem stalled in a bevy of barriers. The extremely competitive reaches of academia and the big city might thereby afford the most obscured viewing of thought contagions.

Competition gets dirty, too, and people learn to be suspicious of each other. Mass beliefs can serve as tools of embezzlement, exploitation, and subjugation; Western history shows their perennial utility for political and military ends. Some would conclude that mass belief exists chiefly as a user-made tool, and seldom as a natural phenomenon. And among those who think this way, thought contagion faces added barriers as a natural phenomenon: even the truest believer finds preaching to the cynical tough. Those regarding mass beliefs as user-made tools thereby become "immune to infection." Among themselves, the cynical naturally have fewer chances to behold self-replicating memes.

Another social barrier to thought contagion, the credential system, provides a method of rejecting important kinds of belief transmission from the uncredentialed. Those holding a doctorate, professional license, or clergy post thereby gain more access to minds than those lacking such distinctions. People do make exceptions, since most are themselves uncredentialed. Yet highly credentialed individuals may apply credential systems more vigorously, limiting the acquisition of common thought contagions among their ranks. Moreover, less credentialed people can recognize the restrictive effects of credential systems well enough that they don't even try to impart beliefs to someone with impressive credentials. All of this helps restrict the circles in which specific thought contagions can travel.

Finally, maturing believers in almost any movement feel increasingly constrained from efforts to persuade others. Many who proselytized openly during young adulthood find that behavior too socially hazardous a decade later. They learn the more cautious approach of one-to-one persuasion at opportune moments, limited to people they know and select carefully. So thought contagions typically slow down and grow less conspicuous in maturing social circles.

All these barriers and slowdowns can certainly make replicator theory appear irrelevant to mass culture, and the inconspicuousness of replication events can make its actual relevance little-noticed by scholars. Yet meme replication need not proceed conspicuously to amass enormous host populations, and the barriers act mainly against proselytism after young adulthood.

A movement spreads quite rapidly if it doubles its population once per decade. While such a rate amounts to a thousand-fold increase per century, the act of making one new convert seldom looks like the event of the decade in anyone's life. The event can take up such a minuscule fraction of a decade's exertions that it commands little attention, even though hugely conspicuous movements grow when populations repeat those events by the millions. Given all the movement's other activities, an outside observer might completely overlook its ten-year retransmitting rate. (See figure 2.)

Yet fast-doubling movements typically gain most of their converts as the young persuade the young. In the Mormon church, for example, believers within young age brackets can average several new converts per decade, while their elders average far fewer. Then, rather than "shedding the beliefs of youth" as outsiders might expect, most of the young converts remain Mormons into old age.

Although most people do stabilize their core beliefs before middle age, those aging youth converts eventually swell their

FIGURE 2

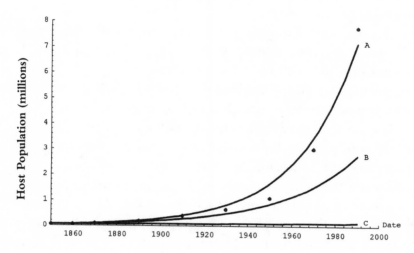

Simulated and Observed Mormon Belief Propagation. Belief replication that looks slow to the casual observer produces one of the fastest-growing movements in the religious world: Dots represent measured Mormon host populations over the past 140 years. Curve A shows simulation results assuming just 1 convert per host per 33 years and 1.2 persuaded offspring per host per lifetime. Curve B shows simulation results assuming the same convert rate with offspring persuasion lowered to a "replacement" level. Curve C simulates the "modest" 2.6-fold growth over 140 years generated by lowering offspring propagations to the commonplace level of 1.2 per host and setting proselytic conversions to 0. *Sources:* Data from the *Encyclopedia of Mormonism*; computation and plotting done with Mathematica software.

ranks among older age brackets. This causes a rapid but delayed doubling of middle-aged Mormons, even though conversions remain sparse at that age.

To mature people witnessing the surge, it may appear that forty-year-olds are simply "becoming more Mormon" or "becoming more religious." No longer situated to scrutinize what belief does for its own replication, these observers may instead ask themselves why so many forty-year-olds are choosing Mormonism. Other observers, such as foreign social scientists, may *never* have lived among young natives, where they could watch and experience the proselytism firsthand. Viewed as outsiders by young locals, they would be spared the conversion attempt altogether.

As for the competitive barriers to proselytism, most believers can avoid them just by limiting their conversion efforts to people who consider them friends—or at least noncompetitors. This does restrict their meme-spreading opportunities, but not severely enough to rule out the few young converts per decade needed for rapid proselytic growth.

If proselytizing the young circumvents a few social barriers to thought contagion, actually raising the young circumvents more. Wherever competition, cynicism, and maturity curtail a meme's proselytic spread, parental growth becomes more important. In the case of the Mormons, population growth in North America results from a combination of high birth rates and high conversion rates. Once again, the beliefs themselves play an important part in their own replication: Mormons believe that in giving birth, they are actually helping premortals advance to a higher life and escape the danger of hell. High birthrates thus take on the status of moral duty to fellow souls.

Some would argue that Joseph Smith was delusional; others would call him a great "inventor" who pursued his projects—accidents and all—not with beakers, but with beliefs. In any case, the Mormon movement he started now has a life of its own, a life carried in memetic replicators.

The barriers to thought contagion do play an important part, preventing most of them from doubling at such wild rates as once a year. Yet the fittest thought contagions have adapted well to a world of barriers, permitting them to gradually amass real power throughout the world.

2

A MISSING LINK: MEMETICS AND THE SOCIAL SCIENCES

"The future belongs to crowds."
—DON DeLILLO

In *The Structure of Scientific Revolutions,* Thomas Kuhn distinguishes between normal science and revolutionary science. In *normal science,* scientists generally build upon the work of others, expanding existing conceptual paradigms to account for more phenomena in more detail. In *revolutionary science,* scientists forsake aspects of existing paradigms and adopt a *paradigm shift* as a new way to understand phenomena.

Memetics represents just such a paradigm shift. In a nutshell, it takes the much explored question of how people acquire ideas and turns it on its head: the new approach often asks how ideas acquire people. More exactly, memetics treats both questions as valid, but finds the new form more useful for some topics, the old form better for others.

To date, social sciences have taken a people-acquiring-ideas perspective for both large- and small-scale phenomena. Many good insights emerged from that vast body of work. But the new insights gained through the ideas-acquiring-people paradigm do not rest firmly on the established science. The scientists who implicitly ask how people acquire ideas design surveys and experiments accordingly, and the resulting data seldom answer the inverted questions of how ideas acquire people. Most hypotheses about how ideas acquire people must remain untested until studies are designed to collect the new forms of data required.

Despite its novel approach, memetics' territory does overlap that of numerous other fields—warranting a look at how memetics relates to specific social sciences. Though the discussion could fill volumes, this introductory work on memetics will provide just an overview of how memetics relates to such fields as economics, sociology, anthropology, sociobiology, evolutionary psychology, political science, communication science, folklore analysis, cognitive psychology, and history.

MEMETICS AND ECONOMICS

Like memetics, economics can measure the success and failure of ideas. Yet the two fields use different yardsticks to measure an idea's fortunes or misfortunes.

Economists typically consider an idea's "success" in terms of how much wealth it accumulates for its adherents. Memetics, on the other hand, measures an idea's success by how much population it accumulates. With "normal" ideas, one expects the most lucrative variants to also become the most populous variants: people simply imitate the ideas of the well-off. For example, when people saw the high productivity of early users of personal computers (PCs), new people kept adopting the ideas until the PC became ubiquitous. In contrast, thought contagions skip the intermediate step of benefiting the adherent as a means to new adherents. Instead, they propagate by manipulating the existing host's communication or reproduction.

By taking this direct route to self-propagation, some movements spread vigorously when measured by population but poorly when measured by wealth. Islamic fundamentalism, for instance, devotes intense effort to spreading and solidifying the faith. Yet solidifying the faith often involves isolationism from Western influence, which hampers investment, trade, and technologic development. These impediments then slow the accumulation of wealth. So the memetic system spreading fast enough to take over a country the size of Iran shows poor growth economically: with its oil exports, Iran could have been a fairly advanced country, but religious isolationism set back its development enormously.

The historic contest between communism and capitalism gives a grander illustration of memes propagating differently in the dimensions of wealth and population. The different economic fates of the two movements arose largely from their different rules of ownership.

Ownership itself is not a meme, because it consists of information stored at the community level. The individual cannot own a car merely by believing she owns the car and driving off with it; a community needs to think she owns the car for her to hold true ownership. Individual owners can even be unaware of what they own, as when babies own money. Because the information resides more at the community than the individual level, ownership qualifies as a kind of "transcendent meme," but not as an ordinary meme.

Rules of ownership, however, are ordinary memes stored in the mind of an individual. One person, for instance, might believe that a tuna caught in international waters belongs to the one who catches it; someone else might believe that all or part of the fish belongs to others.

How much the specific rules spread affects which rules take force on the community level, thus deciding who owns what. How a community reckons ownership in turn governs the incentives for productive behavior. The fisher who gets to keep a fraction of the day's catch feels strongly inclined to raise output, whereas the fisher who gets a constant salary feels little incentive to catch more. The private enterprise rules of ownership thus "program" a society's people to produce more wealth, giving the memes themselves an inherent vigor at raising the amount of wealth the memes govern.

Despite this wealth accretion advantage of private enterprise memes, alternative communist memes have nevertheless enjoyed episodes of faster population growth. Adherents of memes favoring broadly distributed ownership can feel strong incentives to spread those memes. Indeed, people with little property may expect personal gain by spreading socialist or communist beliefs. Naturally, those who would lose wealth under communism feel personally motivated to speak up for private ownership. But when the poor and those feeling poor form a large majority, the communist beliefs can spread faster and farther.

Such was the case in prerevolutionary Russia and China. Communists felt strong economic motives for spreading their belief. Moreover, they often reached sympathetic listeners, allowing the memes to replicate widely. Once the memes spread enough to force a change of rule, the rules of ownership changed too—reducing the production incentives and long-term growth.

Desires to spread the movement persisted long after the first communist governments formed. This allowed communism to propagate on a grander scale: besides individuals replicating their ideologies into new individuals, governments began replicating their ideologies into new governments.

Eventually, however, the widening life-style gap between communist and capitalist countries commanded attention at all levels of society. Individuals in communist countries voiced their discontent to friends and family until anticommunist memes spread widely by "underground" discourse. Even the General Secretary of the Soviet Communist party, Mikhail Gorbachev, adopted a belief in changing the system. Yet once he started the process, a groundswell of memetic and political forces overwhelmed him, ending both the Soviet Union and official Soviet communism.

Unlike the memes of Islamic fundamentalism, communist memes promised greater material prosperity, so when their success at accumulating population met with failure at accumulating wealth, the ideology lost its credibility and appeal. Believers dropped out and persuaded others to drop out.

Yet Russian capitalist memes have also promised greater prosperity, leaving them likewise vulnerable to dropouts during hard times. And the communist legacy fosters hard times by harming the business climate. Old taboos against "profiteering" play a part, hindering or overtaxing investors and causing them to put their money elsewhere. A big Russian mafia compounds the problem. Formed from a giant black market in currencies and consumer goods, it now extorts private companies and scares off potential investors. The resulting disappointment with capitalism has believers dropping out and communists replicating their memes with renewed vigor, keeping communism a potent factor in post Soviet Russia.

MEMETICS AND SOCIOLOGY

Memetics and sociology address closely related topics, examining human behavior from a large-scale perspective. Whereas sociology focuses more attention on the actions of society's groups and structures, memetics concerns itself more with the beliefs that underlie those groups and structures.

The sociologist, for instance, might study a religious denomination's church as an institution, as a social group, or as a hierarchy. If a denomination expands, the sociologist usually asks what sort of advantages attract all the newcomers. The memeticist, on the other hand, studies the denomination's creed with an eye toward how it evolves and furthers its own replication. Although memetics considers personal advantages among the factors that make a movement grow, it avoids tacitly *assuming* that proliferation results from helping adherents or their leaders. As a pragmatic matter, memeticists usually explore the aspects of belief propagation not already covered by sociologists. The two fields thus make their own distinct contributions to understanding religion and other social phenomena.

The memetic perspective also complements the large body of sociology concerning social class formation.

As noted earlier, some rules of ownership do better at the wealth dimension of propagation, and the same point applies to certain ways of judging the value of people. Memes emphasizing wealth as a criterion for reckoning a person's value create an intense drive to accumulate wealth. In a very real sense, hosts of these memes pursue wealth as a means to bettering *themselves.* To gain wealth means to gain self-respect, and to lose wealth means to lose self-respect, according to these memetically coded mental rules. So hosts strive harder for wealth than do other people, and disproportionately congregate in the higher strata of income.

Since the memes suggest measuring nearly everyone's

value by wealth, the hosts also tend to look favorably upon those who are wealthier than they and unfavorably upon those who are poorer. This gives at least one reason for social class segregation: those in a particular wealth bracket tend to hold memes that assign lower value to potential friends in lower wealth brackets. Fortunately for society, few people actually make wealth the *only* criterion for respect.

Those holding wealth-neutral schemes for evaluating themselves and others feel less driven to succeed financially, leaving them disproportionately represented in the average and lower wealth brackets. This includes those who reckon the value of people in terms such as integrity, faith, and knowledge. Those who prize learning illustrate this point: people who measure their merit in terms of knowledge often make excellent students, but the best students less often become the wealthiest adults—despite education's image as a route to economic success.

While memetic reasoning applies to social stratification, it addresses class-neutral types of belief transmission most forcefully. When a meme achieves situation-invariant replication, it stands a better chance of spreading recursively enough to become a mass thought contagion.

In Mormonism, for instance, the idea that conversion saves souls works among numerous economic strata. The faith achieves self-propagation in classes ranging from the poor to the professional, and even the rich. The faith also inspires vigorous procreation across a broad socioeconomic spectrum. Together, these replication advantages make Mormonism America's fastest-growing religion. If the faith had replicative powers only within a limited socioeconomic stratum, then it would lose propagation whenever its hosts moved above or below that stratum. Mormon replication might differ by degrees among classes, but not in its underlying mechanics.

The frequently memetic topics of religion, family, health,

et cetera, do indeed surface in sociological analyses of group and public opinion. These treatments work best for beliefs that play fairly passive roles in their own replication: beliefs that yield the fewest new insights when examined with replicator theory. For instance, the belief that "labor unions benefit the worker" probably derives more propagation from job and pay advantages than from a self-programming replication mechanism—especially now that everyone has heard about unions. Sociologists can therefore ignore replicator theory and focus instead on the performance and interactions of companies, unions, and work forces as determinants of belief propagation. In short, memetics and sociology can both address the prevalence of beliefs, but in some cases the beliefs yield most to sociology's methods, while in other cases they yield most to memetics methods or to a mixture of methods.

MEMETICS AND CULTURAL ANTHROPOLOGY

Cultural anthropology treats beliefs as a subset of human culture, sometimes under the heading of "ideology." Moreover, some anthropologists concentrate on the evolution of culture, including theories about the differential propagation of cultural traits. The anthropologist William H. Durham goes particularly far in this direction, using the meme concept to elucidate the main processes of cultural development in *Coevolution: Genes, Culture, and Human Diversity.* He makes a strong case that prior cultural values predominate in setting the course of subsequent cultural change. In other words, motivational and cognitive receptivity typically determine a meme's fate, and prior memes shape most of the motivation and cognition involved.

Most culture develops through fairly "plain" processes of passive adaptation, and Durham explains this by citing biological evolution: the neural apparatus for sending and receiving culture must make memes adapt to human needs more often than the converse. Otherwise, a culture-ready nervous system would never have evolved and spread in the first place. The argument works for most types of memes, especially over periods of known advancement in cerebral ability. Yet Durham admits that in special circumstances, memes can depart from the mainline route to prevalence. Such "special case" memes are the ones I call *thought contagions.*

Developments over the past few millennia may have made the "special circumstances" supporting thought contagion more common than during most of human evolution. Population densities have soared, and transportation has improved immensely. Just as these factors favor the rampant, even worldwide spread of biological contagions, so too do they favor the spread of thought contagions. People have more communication partners from whom to catch communicable ideas, and more potential retransmitting contacts as well. Modern technology also fosters thought contagion, by putting those potential recipients only a phone call or a broadcast away.

If today's populations indeed have more thought contagions than did prehistoric populations, it may have some impact on the brain's biological evolution. Perhaps it makes the facility for culture less advantageous, thus slowing or even reversing the upward trend in cultural capacity. On the other hand, it may accelerate the brain's evolution of capacities for memetic immunity, pushing it toward more sophisticated levels of cultural capacity. In either case, the changes would happen quite gradually.

Quantity parental memes might even affect genetic evolution differently than would other thought contagions. If a meme causes more reproduction, then genes raising susceptibility to that meme can replicate better. Among the Amish, those with enough cultural capacity to form an "immune reaction" to their native culture and adopt a modern one often drop out. But as a result they have fewer children than the culturally slower Amish they leave behind. This could, with time, shift the Amish gene pool in ways that lower their average capacity to learn modern American culture.

In the broader society, other quantity parental memes may exert similar pressures on biological evolution. Birth control taboos, for instance, require some educability in order to spread but "too much" educability can also hinder transmission by causing people to drop the taboo. So the meme would favor biological evolution to a "compromise" level of learning ability.

When applied to procreation-raising memes, Durham's evolutionary argument that most memes spread passively carries less force. Genetic receptivity to memes that "trick" people into having more descendants is presumably *favored* in biological evolution. Yet practical matters limit the abundance of these memes as a fraction of the total meme pool, consistent with Durham's general statement. Far more memes go into giving people the social and material *ability* to reproduce. Most of *these* memes spread rather passively, consistent with Durham's general statement.

Cultural anthropology takes on thousands of cultures, each one bearing numerous memes. The discipline has a great task analyzing just the usual memetics of culture, and has yet to zero in on the more "exotic" memetics of thought contagion.

In their pursuit of objectivity, anthropologists have traditionally studied cultures foreign to them. Yet in studying thought contagions, added benefit comes from memetic analysis by cultural insiders. Natives can withhold their conversion efforts from outsiders while frequently attempting to convert those regarded as insiders. This would give a memetically trained insider an edge at seeing local beliefs being retransmitted. Still, emotional proximity can blind an insider, and scientifically literate insiders are not available for all cultures. Memetic anthropology could therefore benefit from keeping the outsider perspective and adding more insider perspectives when possible.

In recent decades, the methodology for observing cultural evolution has stirred controversy, but the question of what sort of replicators lay behind that evolution has stirred a hotter controversy—the one surrounding sociobiology.

MEMETICS AND SOCIOBIOLOGY

Before anyone studied cultural behavior's evolution through memetic replicators, biologists studied instinctual behavior's evolution through genetic replicators. Encompassing such diverse human behaviors as aggression, altruism, and family structure, the study emerged under the name *sociobiology*, coined by Edward O. Wilson.

In his famous sociobiology book, *The Selfish Gene,* the evolutionary biologist Richard Dawkins summed up one of the key points of genetic replicator theory: that living organisms are merely the "machines" that genes use to copy themselves into new organisms. Expanding this logic beyond replicating DNA, Dawkins observed that genes are just self-copying information bundles in a storage medium of organic molecules; therefore, some form of neo-Darwinian process must apply to any self-copying information bundles in neural memory, too. He describes this as essentially a human "software" variant of how the "fittest" parasites achieve the widest prevalence among host organisms. To quote from Dawkins's seminal chapter on memes, "When you plant a fertile meme in my mind, you literally parasitize my brain, turning it into a vehicle for the meme's propagation in just the same way that a virus may parasitize the genetic mechanism of a host cell." Information viruses, such as memes, thus follow natural laws like those governing the change and transmission of biological viruses.

Like Durham's later work, Dawkins's thinking allows for both the parasitic and symbiotic behavior of memes, but

Dawkins gives more attention to memes as parasites than does Durham.

In treating culture as a vast swarm of replicators evolving in their own right, both Dawkins and Durham set themselves apart from the school of "hard-line" sociobiologists, whose ideas emerged under the leadership of Edward O. Wilson. Hard-liners regard cultural evolution as fully subordinated to genetic evolution. In *Genes, Mind, and Culture,* Wilson joined Charles Lumsden in proposing that epigenetic rules statistically guide cultural development from each person's genotype. Referring to Dawkins's earlier work, they assail memetic evolution as biologically unfounded. The strictest forms of sociobiology thus clash with memetics, even though Dawkins's moderate version of sociobiology inspired him to launch the memetics.

In recent years, Lumsden and Wilson may have softened their hard-line position. By scaling back its territorial claims in the social sciences, sociobiology should find itself a more solidly defensible role in explaining people's most instinctual behaviors.

EVOLUTIONARY PSYCHOLOGY

Avoiding hard-line extremes while still focusing on genetic evolution, fresh research has emerged under the new heading of evolutionary psychology. The field deals with such topics as innate language propensities and strong emotions, sharing a common interest with memetics in the areas of sex and family life.

In *The Evolution of Desire,* David Buss develops a convincing theory of evolutionary psychology in human mating. The work goes a long way toward explaining numerous details of our partner preferences, love patterns, divorce patterns, and mating strategies. Acknowledging a strong concomitant role for culture, the theory has elements that work well in conjunction with memetics to provide a broad understanding of mating and family behaviors.

A more general survey of evolutionary psychology is presented in Robert Wright's *The Moral Animal*. In addition to looking at the extensive research on mating, Wright examines genetic evolution theories about reciprocal altruism, familial altruism, status hierarchies, and moral self-deception.

Some of the human characteristics attributed to genetic evolution in evolutionary psychology could well turn out to arise from memetic evolution, and vice versa. Other characteristics seem less ambiguously one or the other.

Male sexual jealously, for instance, appears best explained by genetic evolution: by preventing other males from impregnating his mate, a man's genes achieve more replication into the next generation. His memes, on the other hand, can pass on to his mate's children without hindrance from undetected cuckoldry. Evolutionary psychologists seem justified to infer an innate instinct behind male sexual jealousy.

A prevalent female preference for high-status males, however, could derive from genetics, memetics, or both. If high-status men generally enable women to leave more surviving offspring (in the environment of evolutionary adaptation), then either genes or memes specifying that women mate by status should propagate. The memes could become widespread in all human societies for the same reasons the genes could. The relative importance of genes and memes remains to be settled in this case.

Finally, some behavioral characteristics showing reproductive advantage are clearly memetic. The Amish taboo against using modern farm machines, for instance, cannot reside in the genes: it arose too recently and its replication advantage has only existed since the advent of modern machinery.

Memeticists and evolutionary psychologists thus have

their respective domains of theoretical strength. In the future, the two groups of researchers need to sort out the ambiguous areas of human behavior.

MEMES AND POLITICS

Self-sending ideologies permeate the American political scene, and even rival pocketbook issues for top billing. Politically loaded thought contagions will crop up throughout the following chapters, in matters such as abortion, AIDS, religion, sexual morality, and family values. Each replicating ideology presents a potential constituent base, and each political candidate must quilt together enough constituent groups to get elected. Of course, in politics, it matters *who* the believers are and how hard they press their causes. Replicator phenomena churn out an important source of "raw material" for politics. But where the political process takes it from there warrants an entire discipline, known as political science.

What comes out of political processes can in turn affect the spread of that memetic "raw material." Governments, broadcasters, and publishers control the centralized portion of human communication. Yet to curry favor with voters and audiences, those information sources often suit their messages to whatever memes already prevail. Moreover, people mostly "tune out" the distant centralized voices when they expect disagreement. Enough variety exists in the media to allow people to choose a voice of agreement instead. That leaves the power to instill or change strong opinions mostly up to friends and family, the grass-roots sources where thought contagions hold sway.

Grass-roots memes showed their strength clearly in the 1994 Congressional elections, where the Christian Coalition played a key role in turning the outcome to the right. By presenting "moral report cards" on the candidates to millions of devout churchgoers, the coalition exhibited superb election-eering. Yet basic credit must go to the much larger religious movements themselves, for tireless proselytic and parental expansion into a huge bloc. Motivational and proselytic tax-cut memes also played a part, as did a parentally replicated taboo roused by the "gays in the military" issue. So despite a robust economy that by conventional wisdom favored incumbents, liberal incumbents lost heavily to a panoply of replicating beliefs. Thought contagions play a powerful, fundamental role in politics.

COOPERATION GAME THEORY

Without concentrating on opinion per se, the political scientist Robert Axelrod spans levels from the grass roots to geopolitics in his work on cooperation theory. His essentially memetic investigations have culminated in his book *The Evolution of Cooperation*. Using computer simulations, Axelrod shows how relatively "nice" life strategies such as "tit for tat" can outpros-per and outreplicate the "nasty" strategies—even in an unregu-lated, survival-of-the-fittest world. He goes on to apply the results to real-life situations, and explores some of the compli-cations that arise from social reality. The book makes excellent reading for memetically minded thinkers.

Following Axelrod's work, new research explores the evo-lution of cooperation with increasingly sophisticated computer simulations. One pair of scientists, Martin Nowak and Karl Sigmund, advanced the field significantly in an article they published in *Nature*. By simulating a population of selfish agents that reproduce, "mutate," make occasional mistakes, and recall two sides of a prior transaction, they found high levels of coop-eration evolving by a win–stay, lose–shift strategy they call *Pavlov.*

If a win–stay, lose–shift mentality carries over to broader

contexts, it could favor new outbreaks of proselytic movements during hard times. Anyone who feels that he or she is "losing" could become more inclined to shift from long-held beliefs. When many people feel this way, that creates an opportunity for proselytic beliefs to spread recursively through a "susceptible" population. Hard times can thus explain cases of wide susceptibility, while proselytic intensity explains which movements win the lion's share of new converts.

MEMETICS AND COMMUNICATION SCIENCE

The communication scientist Everett M. Rogers considers still another form of differentially spreading information in *The Diffusion of Innovations*. Focusing on technologies and other pragmatic matters, Rogers reveals a number of factors affecting how far and fast an innovation spreads. Any increased benefit of the new way over the old hastens its spread, as does compatibility with a community's existing values. If people can easily try the innovation on a limited basis, or easily observe others doing so, it also spreads faster. Too much complexity, on the other hand, slows the meme's transmission, an observation that applies to ideological thought contagions as well.

As the word *diffusion* suggests, Rogers treats memes that play mostly passive roles in their own transmission. When potential adopters evaluate an innovation for its benefits, compatibility, simplicity, and trialability, they retain great control over the meme.

Strains of thought contagion do emerge, however, in the observability part of Rogers's theory, because some innovations self-advertise better than others. Rogers gives the example of solar panels on household roofs in California. Everyone who adopts the innovation puts up a virtual "billboard advertisement" on the rooftop, and this provokes queries and imitation by others.

In the area of fashion, innovations often self-advertise by mere novelty to the current populace: a style not seen in recent memory catches the eye better, boosting the rate of imitation. That makes adopting the style more enticing to attention seekers, and better noticed by many others. Once the style achieves prevalence, it grabs less attention, setting the stage for the next style to capture attention and spread. Of course, fashion moguls play their part, as do society's social divisions. Yet fashions, solar panels, and other conspicuous trends do illuminate the category of "self-diffusing" innovations as a subclass of thought contagions.

FOLKLORE AS THOUGHT CONTAGION

The popular series of books by the folklorist Jan Harold Brunvand explores still another subtype of thought contagion: the urban legend. Usually bizarre, horrible, or funny, urban legends are those plausible narratives regarded as true by most tellers and listeners—but generally found to be mythical after careful investigation. Stories about sexual practices, involving gerbils, elephants sitting on Volkswagens, toilets exploding, et cetera, fill the pages of Brunvand's four books.

While Brunvand examines the psychological meanings of these stories, the stories also demonstrate a self-contagious principle: vivid, gripping stories are retold. When a story grips the imagination, people cannot stop thinking about it. That alone makes them mention it more often to new listeners. When the new listeners hear it, they give the story—and the reteller—their rapt attention. Since most people crave attention, they enjoy retelling the story and therefore do so repeatedly. So the stories spread, to the point where almost everyone hears them.

The urban legend that McDonald's restaurants had replaced ground beef with ground earthworms in hamburgers illustrates some of these points. On the psychological level, Brunvand shows how the rumor plays upon deep fears of contamination. Yet it also captures the imagination and draws rewarding attention to those who retell it—a more actively thought-contagious effect. Finally, those who hear the rumor feel motivated to warn others about those worms in the food. This they do by revoicing the urban legend, completing the cycle of meme manipulating host to respread meme.

As the parlor game "telephone" demonstrates, recursive storytelling in a large group generates numerous variations from the original version. If any of these variants is more vivid and gripping, it is retold more often than the original, and eventually out-propagates it. As the new variant receives more and more tellings, its chances of "mutating" to a still more contagious strain go up, and so forth. By the time the stories reach mass circulation, they may have outdone many previous versions, and become nearly optimized for stimulating their own repetitions. In short, thought contagions and Darwinian selection hold the makings of an urban legend.

The prevalence of urban legends creates a broad market for Brunvand's books, and an even wider mention of his ideas in urban gatherings. As Brunvand notes, there emerges a folklore about folklorists, and perhaps even urban legends about urban legends. The whole topic becomes self-referential, like memetics applied to the spread of memetics itself.

MEMES IN COGNITIVE SCIENCE AND PHILOSOPHY OF MIND

Douglas R. Hofstadter and Daniel C. Dennett gave the "memetics meme" a dissemination boost in the fields of cognitive science, philosophy of mind, and artificial intelligence. In 1981 they included some of Dawkins's work in their book, *The Mind's I*. By then, Hofstadter had already explored self-referential systems and self-referential sentences in *Gödel, Escher, Bach: An Eternal Golden Braid,* and was continuing the discourse in his monthly *Scientific American* column. The exposure to Dawkins eventually led them to publish their own contributions in memetics.

When Hofstadter's "Metamagical Themas" column in the January 1982 *Scientific American* revisited the subject of self-referential sentences, it sparked two readers to write letters relating self-replicating and self-referential sentences. The letters formed the starting point for Hofstadter's 1983 column "On Viral Sentences and Self-Replicating Structures."

Stephen Walton's letter draws chain letters into the discussion, noting how they generally promise rewards for resending and punishments for "breaking the chain." Walton coined the phrase *viral text* for such items as chain letters, and *viral sentence* for the statements they contain.

Donald Going's letter brings up the hell idea, noting how it self-replicates by motivating believers to "save" the "unsaved" from eternal torment. He goes on to discuss a more general "sentence V," which states (in one way or another), "The Villain is wronging the Victim." By replacing the format words *Villain* and *Victim* with specific names, one arrives at some of the actual political memes of history. The *Villain* can refer to "capitalists," "communists," "Jews," and so forth; *Victim* refers to the groups allegedly harmed.

Hofstadter's column goes on to the topics of indirect self-reference and indirect self-replication. This leads from real-life memes to sentences that self-document and even "self-replicate" by way of typographical statements and commands. Though atypical of memes, the sentences make playfully imaginative denizens in the "biosphere" of words. Hofstadter's column and a "Post Scriptum" appear in his 1985 book, *Metamagical Themas.*

In *Consciousness Explained,* Daniel C. Dennett develops a

plausible theory that consciousness itself arises from the workings of a great "software" package "installed" in our brains by those who raise and educate us. The software consists of numerous memes specifying how to think, giving us our mental lives almost as surely as disk software imparts functions to a personal computer.

Much as computer viruses make up a small fraction of computer software, so too do pernicious thought contagions form a small part of all our mental software. As Dennett puts it:

> We would not survive unless we had a better-than-chance habit of choosing the memes that help us. Our meme-immunological systems are not foolproof, but not hopeless either. We can rely, as a general, crude rule of thumb, on the coincidence of the two perspectives: by and large, the good memes are the ones that are also the good replicators.
>
> The theory becomes interesting only when we look at the exceptions, the circumstances under which there is a pulling apart of the two perspectives; only if meme theory permits us better to understand the deviations from the normal scheme will it have any warrant for being accepted. (p. 205)

As a philosopher of mind explaining the nature of consciousness, Dennett mainly considers the kind of memes that spread symbiotically, the ones that help us think correctly and adapt to our environments. Natural selection, he says, usually favors the most effective "problem-solving" memes. People like to imitate those memes, and these memes can also boost their host's survival and reproduction.

Memes that spread purely by acting as efficient replicators remain tangential to the broader study of consciousness, and Dennett therefore treats these important special-case memes briefly in *Consciousness Explained*. He does, however, revisit the subject of memes in his 1995 book, *Darwin's Dangerous Idea*. Within this broad and important affirmation of evolution theory, Dennett turns part of his attention to Darwinian evolution in the *infosphere*, arguing for continued development of memetics as a science.

MEMETIC HISTORY

Modern historiography already branches into the histories of ideas, knowledge, inventions, and religions. Memetics, on the other hand, is a theory of *how* history unfolds, one pertaining to the history of mass belief. Memetics also seeks to explain the form and prevalence of current beliefs, and how these might change in the future.

The situation resembles the analogous relationship between the evolution theory and the discipline of paleontology, where paleontology parallels historiography and evolution theory parallels memetics theory. Though evolution refers to biological history, it cannot incorporate a full account of that history. Likewise, memetics cannot incorporate a full account of human history.

Both memetic evolution and genetic evolution also explain some historic transitions more directly than others. Few scientists would use genetic evolution to understand the mass extinctions following a large meteor impact, and few would use thought contagion theory to explain America's sudden shift to a war mentality when Japan bombed Pearl Harbor. In both cases, history's great events cause changes beyond those that evolving replicators produce.

Yet as more biologists discover the importance of the planet's great events, modern historians increasingly study how great trends arise from billions of history's "little people" and "little events." This expansion beyond the "great man" paradigm works well with memetics. The powerful frequently do command belief disseminations, but often a belief spreads first and gains powerful proponents later. Memetics offers its fresh insights into this latter phenomenon, and leaves most study of historical figures to biographers and historians.

Memetics's focus on beliefs as replicators can likewise give short shrift to prominent people. To multiply aggressively, memes must affect large numbers of people in similar ways. But most of any large crowd consists of "little people," so the theory cannot ignore them in favor of prominent people.

Even in its focus on "little people," memetics pays disproportionate attention to our more benign and unsophisticated communications. The seemingly little events of communication greatly outnumber the big ones, and are easier to imitate. So they play an important role in mass movements.

The best replicators command retransmitting behaviors from adherents great and small, over wide areas, and across long time spans. Prominent figures may do more meme spreading per person, but the common folk often account for most of a meme's replication through their sheer numbers. Once again, the history of thought contagion calls less attention to great players than do other branches of history.

MEMETICS AND PSYCHOHISTORY

Some have likened memetic history to the science fiction account of a theory called "psychohistory" in Isaac Asimov's *Foundation* series. Although psychohistory did not inspire memetics, the two theories do have surprising similarities. Both theories concern *how* history unfolds, and both give more consideration to the cumulative behavior of great masses than to the actions of special individuals. Both theories can cover hundreds of generations, and both can be translated into quantitative, mathematical equations. Like psychohistory, the memetic equations can even predict "future history" given some well-measured parameters and starting conditions.

Yet the analogies start to fade from that point on. In the science fiction story, a psychohistorian can predict most of society's behavior far into the future and quite precisely. Thought contagion theory mainly considers a special subclass of ideological behaviors, and just measuring the variables can raise serious practical challenges. The quantitative translation of the theory also leads to nonlinear equations, which mathematicians and meteorologists now see as a bane to long-range forecasting.

Thought contagion memetics might never equal the stuff of science fiction, but it can make an important contribution to the understanding of history and the human condition.

3

FAMILY PLANS: IDEAS THAT WIN WITH CHILDREN

The hand that rocks the cradle is the hand that rules the world.
—WILLIAM ROSS WALLACE

Values about family structure affect how many offspring we raise, and how well they imitate their parents. Meanwhile, a long history of genetic evolution apparently gives us such biological emotions as romantic love, sexual desire, jealousy, love for children, and a preference for offspring over stepchildren. The field of evolutionary psychology studies these innate emotions and their impact on family structures. Memetics, on the other hand, studies cultural orientations that also exert enormous force in shaping family life.

THE FAMILY OPTION

The most basic family decision is whether to pursue family life at all. Parental replication favors a widespread yes to this question. Many feel that if they can start a family, they should. These people, on average, transmit their family values to more children than those who hold indifferent or avoidant family values. Compounded over generations, the effect insures that a majority of the population becomes family-minded. Yet nonhosts of the family meme stay well above extinction, even if they never raise children: no matter how many children the family-minded raise, some fraction of the children do not imitate their parents' values. If this fraction is, for example, 20 percent of the children, then the adult population must always contain at least 20 percent nonfamily types.

The proportion who do imitate their parents, on the other hand, constitute the family meme's *imitation ratio*. Natural selection generally favors high imitation ratios, since well-imitated memes outpropagate poorly imitated ones.

Still, achieving high imitation ratios sometimes clashes with achieving the high fertility rates also favored by natural selection. If parents have more children than they can comfortably raise, a higher fraction of them may grow up regarding parenthood as an unpleasant experience. This apparently happened for many baby boomers, who registered record levels of women who intend to remain childless. So family-mindedness spreads by favoring reproduction, but loses propagation when it promotes too much reproduction. Evolution apparently favors some level of moderation.

Factors other than whether the parents appear to be struggling or having fun affect imitation ratios. Imitation rates depend on details of family structure and specific styles of raising children. Hence these, too, obey forces of evolution by natural selection.

LOVE FOR CHILDREN

One very simple determinant of imitation ratio is the degree to which children feel loved by their parents. A child who feels loved can more easily believe that her parents spread ideas to her for her own good. The child who persistently feels unloved by his parents, however, may conclude that the parents dictate values mainly for their own self-interests rather than the child's interests. That notion tends to make children reject their parents' examples and teachings. So the belief that "parents should show love for their children" spreads by enhancing imitation rates, including the rate for the "love your kid" meme itself.

That enhanced imitation also extends to helping parents pass down their family-mindedness, resulting in more grand-children for the parents who loved their children. Indeed, child-love ideas enhance the parental-mode transmission of all sorts of memes, leading to all sorts of indirect propagation advantages. For example, the taboo against birth control can enjoy higher imitation rates in well-loved children, who more often accept that the taboo is taught for their own good.

"Love for children" memes can enhance fertility rates in simple, direct ways, too. Those who love children, or who *think* they do, may have more of them on average than those who don't. This would give the meme still more reproductive vigor. With all its intensity and prevalence, the belief even garners proselytic expression in the form of "Have you hugged your kid today?" stickers.

Biological evolution greatly preceded memetic evolution in producing an instinctive parental love for children. Yet these instincts sometimes fail, creating another niche for memetic evolution.

NON–NUCLEAR FAMILY STRUCTURES

Clans of many parents raising children jointly constitute the world's most non–nuclear families. Though such arrangements differ from the norms of prevailing Eurasian and American culture, they proliferated for many centuries in sub–Saharan Africa. Members of these clans owned land collectively before Western rule, and adults could mate freely with people other than their spouses.

The clan–as–family meme reduced the effect of economic motives in limiting fertility. Children with many siblings received the same share of the clan's food as children with few siblings. So the cost to an adult of having one more child was diluted among all clan members, promoting many children per adult. Moreover, the sexually open marriages made sure that women who could become pregnant did so. The meme set thus achieved enough replication vigor to predominate in much of precolonial Africa.

MONOGAMY AND THE NUCLEAR FAMILY

The Eurasian family structure evolved an early trend toward the "nuclear family." The most "nuclear" structure, called *biparental,* holds both biological parents responsible for a child's upbringing. True biparentalism relies on committed sexual monogamy, which ensures that the biological father becomes the child's familial father. Monogamy also supports biparentalism by preventing a paternity dispute that can leave the child with no familial father at all. Adding long-term commitment removes the chance that couples will break up during the predetection phase of pregnancy, again keeping the biological father around to act as family father.

This nuclear family meme set creates economic motives for retransmitting to offspring and other relatives. Those holding themselves responsible for their own biological children usually wish to avoid adding other people's children to the burden, especially unexpectedly. Doing so would give them an "unfair" share of the community's reproductive cost, thus lowering their economic status. But single or premature parenthood of close kin virtually forces them into extra child-raising costs. Preventing these surprise kin costs thus becomes a matter of persuading kin to likewise handle their own reproductive expenses. One meets the kin-expense threat by retransmitting nuclear family memes forcefully to daughters, sisters, and nieces, and somewhat less forcefully to sons, brothers, and nephews. The sex bias results from the women's naturally greater risk of single parenthood, but nuclear family memes still advance by kin persuasion in both sexes.

Although nuclear family members feel economic motives to prevent relatives from turning to the extended family for child support, members of ancient collective families would have felt no similar motive to stop relatives from "going nuclear." The nuclear family meme package thus held at least one advantage at out-propagating the alternative memes.

Yet the nuclear family's emphasis on committed monogamy tends to delay reproduction until after a spouse search—a definite disadvantage in the population race against collective family structures. To achieve its historically strong replication advantage over collective families, biparentalism must have also promoted fertility.

One fertility advantage of biparentalism arises from memetic diversity among its adherents. Biparentalism propagates by ensuring that the people whose mating behavior produces the most children also raise those children personally. That is, among biparentalists, the parents with the strongest bundles of quantity parental memes are the ones imparting ideas to the most children.

Monogamy further ensures that high fertility fathers are

the fathers who do the most child raising. Without biparental-ism and monogamy, children can be raised and influenced more by adults who hold few or no quantity parental memes.

For instance, without monogamous biparentalism, men with taboos against interrupted intercourse would not raise all the extra children that result from their taboo. Instead, although they produced more children than average, they might only make an average contribution to their society's collective child-raising effort.

But in the monogamous biparental population, taboo hosts would do a disproportionate share of the child raising, leading to increasing taboo prevalence in successive generations and thus increasing fertility rates for monogamous biparental-ism as well. The same shifting representation would favor all the population's quantity parental memes at once, leading to a dras-tic combined advantage for monogamous biparentalism.

From the children's perspective, each child has a certain *fertility heritage* consisting of all those memes affecting the par-ents' fertility rate. Imagine two tribes starting with identical fer-tility rate distributions but dissimilar family structures. The cou-pled tribe has a biparental arrangement, while the collective tribe has a highly shared parental arrangement giving all adults equal child-raising responsibility. Mathematically, the average child in the coupled tribe has a provably higher fertility her-itage than the average child in the collective, even though the tribes' adults start with identical fertility distributions.

On growing up, children with a high fertility heritage pre-sumably show a high adult fertility rate. So in the next genera-tion, the average fertility in the biparental group shifts upward while it remains constant in the other group. The differences become greater and greater in successive generations until the biparental group suffers lost imitation ratios among overbur-dened parents. From then on, the biparental group tends to remain near its reproductive limit but still outpopulates the other group by growing margins.

Nuclear families also proliferate because most monogamous couples can only realize the benefits of children by having their own. Such benefits include the manual labor value of children throughout much of history, as well as their emotional benefit to those who love children. In a sufficiently extended family setting, some adults share these benefits without having their own children. By reducing that sharing, the nuclear family arrangement discourages voluntary childlessness. It thereby pulls up its own adherents' fertility norm. The extra fertility again helps the nuclear family to outpopulate its more extended family alternatives.

A nuclear structure can also enhance imitation ratios by reducing conflicting influences in child raising. The more adults raising a child, the more likelihood that they contradict each other. Presented with conflicting values, the child must decide which adult to believe, and may choose to imitate none of them. This independent thinking may generalize to erode imitation of even those memes the adults all hold in common. By minimizing the number of adults raising a child, the biparental system cuts down that kind of imitation loss. The transmission efficiency in turn helps impart any quantity parental memes the parents have, giving a twofold boost to the spread of nuclear family structure.

MARRIAGE

Among the oldest and most common customs in the world, marriage can be analyzed from both memetic and biological perspectives.

On the biological side, several advantages emerge for the two sexes. That men should require permanent commitment from women follows as a corollary to male sexual jealously: men pass on more genes by keeping their women away from other men. Requiring commitment from men follows from the theory of male parental investment: obligating a man to stay and help raise the children improves their odds of survival, spreading both the man's and the woman's genes to more descendants.

On the memetic side, the exclusion of other males from a man's partner becomes less relevant. But the survival argument carries equal force: keeping both parents involved in their children's survival spreads memes down to more descendants than would a noncommittal scheme that leaves children poorly supported.

Yet the memetic replication advantages of marriage go beyond a mere parallel to the genetic survival story. Although men can sometimes pass their genes along by copulating with and deserting women, they never pass their memes along this way. Indeed, the women they leave behind may specifically instruct the children *not* to be like their fathers. Men who stay involved with their children, however, gain lasting chances to pass their beliefs into the next generation. Inasmuch as marriage and commitment keep more men involved with their children, the *belief* in marriage should thus get more replication per male host than alternative beliefs. With enough generations of father-to-son meme transmission, the belief in marriage ensures itself wide prevalence in the male population.

On the female side, strong marriage memes allay fears of desertion by making it illegal. Assured of having at least one man around to help feed the children, married women feel more willing to reproduce than do unmarried women. The consequently abundant children then receive those marriage memes from their parents. Strong marriages thereby retransmit the belief in strong, mandatory marriages.

Finally, kin persuasion enters the picture for marriage

memes much as it does for monogamy memes. The parents, aunts, uncles, siblings, and friends of a young woman retransmit marriage memes to her as a way to prevent the material and emotional cost of poorly supported children from passing along to them.

All these routes to replication leave little wonder that marriage became a centerpiece of family life throughout the world.

POLYGAMOUS MARRIAGE

All the replication advantages of marriage per se do not dictate how many husbands a woman can have or how many wives a man can have. Again, genetic evolutionists have weighed in on the issue, explaining that polygyny should prevail over polyandry because men's genes gain more reproduction from multiple wives than women's genes gain from multiple husbands. One man can impregnate many women whereas multiple men add little to the birth rate of one woman.

The argument certainly explains the different erotic appeal of multiple partners to the two sexes. Differing innate drives can in turn explain the different actions of men and women regarding polygamy.

As a cultural phenomenon, marriage itself remains subject to propagating moral codes. Behaving like genes, propolygamy ideas should enjoy wider prevalence in men than in women because men gain more parental *belief* replication from polygyny than women gain from polyandry. Polygyny memes can even outpopulate monogamous marriage memes under some demographic and economic conditions. In highly stratified societies, for instance, polygyny boosts reproduction by keeping virtually all fertile women married to men who can afford the children.

Polygyny memes fare much worse at proselytism. When men look for a mate, they prefer to see competing men take as few women as possible. So regardless of how many wives they want for themselves, they would rather tell unrelated men to limit themselves to one. Meanwhile, men find more reason to *avoid* promoting polygyny to their competitors, and men who seek multiple wives find perhaps the most reason for not proselytizing. This gives the monogamous marriage meme a proselytic advantage among men, and probably accounts for its central position in family life.

NUCLEAR FAMILY WEALTH

Besides spreading farther and wider than competing schemes, the nuclear family also has advantages at upward social propagation. Nuclear families allow wealth to concentrate by preventing its wide sharing among members of a big collective. Though not *productive* of wealth, this "keeping it in the family" concentrates wealth in nuclear families more easily than in large clan arrangements. Moreover, through kin persuasion, nuclear family members limit their odds of supporting any more children than immediate offspring. The proportion of nuclear family memes in wealthy settings should thus exceed the proportions found in poor settings.

By helping the individual producer to keep and concentrate wealth, the nuclear family may also raise the production *incentive* beyond what it was in the clan structure. Likewise, the nuclear setting raises the punishments for nonproduction, since the unproductive face less chance of survival, mating, and viable reproduction in a community of nuclear families. By both the carrot and the stick, the nuclear meme thus pressures its adherents into maintaining at least one producer per couple. Although clan members may face great social pressures to produce, more urgent pressures may cause greater production per capita in nuclear families. This gives nuclear family memes the twofold advantage of wealth production and concentration, advancing its propagation in socioeconomic dimensions.

By achieving high prevalence in high places, the nuclear family meme attracts more imitators, further helping its spread in the "horizontal," or populational, dimension.

FAMILY HOMES

Long recognized for its utility as both shelter and social statement, the single-family house also serves as an economic bond between mates. Because it usually requires a big investment, neither spouse, whether breadwinner or homemaker, can readily forfeit the house to leave a mate and offspring. This gives both partners an added sense that no matter what goes wrong in their relationship, each will stay around to help with child raising and support. Dependent homemakers, in particular, will worry less that a highly employable husband would depart for a new job and a new life far away. By helping to prevent this disaster, the house's settling influence—much like the effect of marriage—makes couples feel more secure about reproduction.

The more money a couple spends on joint real estate, the more confident they can feel in each other's commitment to stay settled together. Extra children resulting from this mutual confidence can partly explain the proliferation of plans to buy as large a house as the income allows. Furthermore, a spacious house removes domestic crowding as a disincentive to having many children. Indeed, the larger the house, the more children a couple need just to make it feel fully occupied. Finally, home ownership can help singles attract a mate, thus contributing to their reproductive success. All this reproductive drive helps spread the desire for a big, single-family house.

The house-size and family-size connection can also work in reverse. Having many children motivates couples to seek larger houses when finances permit. Even couples who initially lack a big-house meme may thus adopt the meme to meet changing circumstances. Alternatively, they may acquire a big-house meme by imitating other couples with large families. Either way, their children can imitate this preference by observing the parents' example or by hearing them voice their values. Such children can thus receive the big-house meme long before they need to house their own children. And if couples with large families indeed gravitate into large houses, the average large home owner becomes imitated by more children than does the average small home owner. The big-house meme even gets itself "packaged" along with all the other quantity parental memes transmitted in typical big families. So the big-house meme passively acquires another quantity parental advantage.

Single-family houses also intensify the biparental family structure by separating the children of each couple from the parental influences of other couples. Two sets of parents sharing the same living quarters would probably influence each other's children more than would separately quartered parents. Such a multiparental upbringing would lower the children's mean fertility heritage, as mentioned earlier. Couples can also obey the monogamy meme more easily in single-family homes. So along with all its other functions, the single-family home helps keep the nuclear family nuclear.

SINGLE PARENTHOOD

Despite all its strengths in times past, the two-parent system of child raising meets an increasingly viable challenge from the one-parent system in modern times. Several aspects of modern civilization enable mothers in particular to go it alone, often without even considering marriage. Perhaps the earliest such element was free public education, which offered the tacit benefit of free day care for children six to eighteen years old. A second element was a workplace transformed in ways that allowed greater employment for women, permitting many to support children without a husband. Public and private safety nets act to further lower the survival risks for these single mothers.

Still another factor making single parenthood viable is the enhanced support role it gives to grandparents who accept the system. Biparental families usually separate from one or both sets of grandparents, especially where industrialization forces couples to move for employment reasons—usually the husband's job. Yet staying unattached to any one man gives a woman greater freedom to stay with her mother, who can then help with child raising. The arrangement works better when the grandmothers are themselves single mothers with no regrets about it. Although grandmothers usually offer less support than a *working* husband does, they actually make *better* coproviders in communities with high male unemployment. Increasing life spans also improve their value at long-term care and support for the grandchildren.

Single parenthood further propagates by shortening the time needed to start a family. Women who skip the long, uncertain ordeal of finding a suitable husband can start reproduction as early as their teens. This puts their growth on a faster exponential than equally maternal women who delay maternity to find a husband. Women who skip the husband search can also lower the odds of remaining childless, once again giving their value system a replication edge. It all adds up to a conspicuous and controversial trend among today's families.

GENDER ROLES

Evolutionary forces shape family structure from starting sizes and bonding schemes to gender roles of parents and children. Some gender roles, such as pregnancy and infant nursing, are set biologically. Moreover, biology provides average women with certain aptitudes different from those of average men. Yet sexual biology still leaves memetic forces to settle most role differences. Those culturally specified role differences often result from memes advancing themselves through fertility gains for their own hosts.

The "male breadwinner and female dependent" custom thrives on just such a fertility advantage. The custom consists of role identity memes along with beliefs in the superiority of men as breadwinners and of women as homemakers. A good evolutionary model for these memes must explain why they were once widespread norms and why their prevalence has dropped in recent decades. Parental replication first in primitive economies and later in modern economies accounts for the rise and fall of the "traditional" single-income household.

The domestic wife role prevailed partly by affecting the incentives for and against pregnancy. Pregnancy to a woman expecting to remain a homemaker poses no threat of lost food or wages. That presumably makes pregnancy seem more convenient, and hence more frequent for hosts of the domestic wife meme.

Conversely, having children—especially in quantity—creates domestic demands that motivate well-situated women to leave the formal work force. The logic connecting large families to the domestic wife role thus resembles the big-family, big-house logic: even women who initially reject the domestic wife meme can end up playing a domestic maternal role. This exposes the children to a domestic wife idea long before they grow up to experience the time demands of having their own children. If the most reproductive women gravitate into the domestic role, it raises the number of children exposed to full-time domestic wives. This gives a passive parental advantage to the domestic wife meme. It also helps the meme by spreading it selectively within families who already have other parentally vigorous memes.

The physiology of fertility also helps shape work roles of women. Recent research finds a positive correlation between women's fertility and their fat-to-lean ratio. Fertility onset depends on females' developing sufficient body fat during adolescence, and its continuation depends on maintaining a certain body fat proportion. Vigorous physical work tends to burn off fat and build muscle, both of which reduce the fat-to-lean ratio and hence fertility. Historical economies involved more physically demanding jobs and fewer sedentary ones. So the fat-linked fertility effect would have conferred parental advantage to the domestic wife meme back in those days.

Still, this fertility-based propagation gives way to preservational forces in the world's poorest regions. The biological linkage between fattiness and fertility evolved genetically as insurance that a woman became pregnant only after she stored enough calories to carry gestation to term. Pregnancy without assured food and body fat could waste all the calories spent on a partially finished pregnancy while posing a risk to the mother's life. So hard physical labor by very poor women can cut the fertility rate to the point where the fewer pregnancies that occur are sustainable ones. Surviving famished sterility episodes to leave a few offspring beats dying childlessly in all modes of meme replication. The products of women's labor also determine survival much more under poor conditions, but here the survival motive provides work incentive with or without gender customs.

In prosperous lands, fat-linked fertility created a replication advantage for memes enjoining females from heavy labor in many settings, such as their parents' farms. Sons were considered more employable on the farm than were daughters. The delayed fertility resulting from a daughter doing hard farm work would have shortened daughters' reproductive span, cutting transmission of their work memes down to granddaughters. So the idea of similar labor for sons and daughters would have quietly lost its replication race against the more sexist memes that prevailed. Against this background, parents eventually came to see daughters as an economic liability.

The "economic liability" led to the practice of offering a dowry to the man who would eventually take her support out of parental hands. Daughters could actually have been more affordable to parents who practiced the dowry custom than to those who didn't, since those who didn't could end up supporting the daughters further into their adulthood. Moreover, the dowry lets a daughter start reproduction earlier, in the high-fertility role of a domestic wife. Couples would also be willing to have more children, particularly daughters, if they believed that they could limit the expense of supporting a daughter to the cost of raising her plus the dowry cost. So the dowry thrives on both motivational (economic) and parental modes in a society where women stay home with children while men labor physically for support.

BABY DOLLS FOR GIRLS AND HERO DOLLS FOR BOYS

Along with role memes for male and female come specific child-raising memes to instill them. These include some very powerful memes governing the kinds of play that parents promote in young children. Girls, for instance, can play "house," and boys can play in make-believe forts.

Children's toys also fall under strong memetic control, especially in the kinds of dolls they can have. The meme specifying that baby dolls go to girls runs so strong that violators risk serious sanctions. For boys, the memes emphasize hero dolls, soldier dolls, and their antagonists.

The "baby doll for girls" meme replicates partly by training females to play the domestic role that leads to more children for them. Parents who give baby dolls to their daughters thus have their memes imparted to more grandchildren.

Early practice with a doll might foster the gentle nurturing that helps females perform well as real mothers, too. This would also help the meme replicate into more surviving offspring, accounting for still more of its prevalence.

The meme may also have emotional effects lasting long after childhood, increasing women's desire to have real babies. During girlhood, the baby doll provides a source of comfort and make-believe attachment. As the girl grows up, she learns that she is too old to play with dolls anymore. But the desire for comfort and attachment remains, and translates into desire for a real baby. Seeing other women enjoy comfort and attachment from a real baby heightens the desire still further, to a point sometimes called "baby lust" in contemporary America. The new little girls wind up cuddling baby dolls of their own, and the cycle repeats. Females taught to seek the comfort and attachment of a tiny companion therefore outpopulate females taught otherwise.

Desires to have children also replicate parentally in males. Yet to have the maximum number of offspring, most males must learn to distance themselves from babies long enough to go out and provide the material support. Hence, the taboo against play and attachment with baby dolls holds a replication edge in the male population.

Memes that favor hero dolls for boys spread more effectively—partly by displacing baby dolls and partly by providing early role training. The dolls help boys fantasize about going out in the world and conquering, a role that broadly resembles what they must do to attract a mate and provide for children later on. Memes for giving such dolls to boys thus get themselves replicated into more descendants than alternative memes, explaining their wide prevalence today.

Similar learning of adult roles can happen with the grown woman dolls that girls receive in addition to their baby dolls. These dolls typically emphasize feminine beauty, which matters greatly in the girl's mating success later on. Memes for giving "beautiful woman" dolls to girls might thus enhance their own retransmission into the next generation by telling little girls how to win a husband later. The dolls of youth are serious toys, with serious roots in memetic evolution.

WOMEN EMPLOYED

Today's economy mainly provides sedentary jobs, somewhat changing the replication advantages for different role memes.

Fat-linked fertility, for instance, no longer favors the domestic wife meme as it once did. Modern countries typically combine sedentary work with abundant food that doubles the fat content of ancient foods. So a woman's body fat seldom falls below the fertility threshold with or without a domestic role. That change alone is enough to reduce the prevalence of the domestic wife meme. Evolution simply drifts away from the products of obsolete replication advantages.

Other factors have no doubt accelerated women's entry into the work force. Couples can feel more willing to have children when each one prepares to support herself throughout adulthood. The possibility of having a permanently unmarried daughter can deter a couple from having children if the daughter cannot support herself as a single adult. And with finding a husband less urgent for the employable daughter, a marriage-hastening dowry drops out of the cost of having daughters. So the belief in career-track education for both daughters and sons can outreplicate older attitudes by making reproduction look more affordable. In a well-fed sedentary work force, that replication advantage remains unspoiled by hard labor's toll on female fertility.

In a matter of simple economic decision making, parents also switch from old-fashioned to modern ideas about raising their daughters. With "acceptably" sedentary jobs open to women, parents see economic benefits to themselves and their daughters for developing marketable skills. The advent of publicly funded education for both sexes helped the decision along by lowering the parents' cost of providing marketable skills. When based solely on economic considerations, memetic change operates about as fast as the schools and workplaces change, without requiring generations of replication. This fast motivational confluence with slower parental-mode change in the "employable woman" meme allows women's entry into the work force to persist over generations instead of slowly dying out from replication failure.

Still, modern economies retain a replication niche for the domestic wife meme. The inconvenience of pregnancy for career women remains. School and day care eliminate some of the inconvenience, but the services still present a cost deterrent against reproduction in double-income households but not in male breadwinner households. And the less money a working mother makes, the less her wages can justify the cost of day care, especially for multiple children. So the traditional homemaker role still has replication strength, especially with affluent husbands. The greatest replication might favor the belief that women should pursue careers while striving to become traditional wives of men who can support them and their children.

Acquisition of job skills by women can show another replication advantage among women living the traditional wife role. Traditional couples can regard the wife's employability as a fallback position for harder times. That extra security can relieve couples' worries about the discretionary expense of reproduction. This tends to bring more children to couples with highly employable wives than to those with marginally employable wives.

The different work role memes, in turn, affect the institution of marriage. The male breadwinner and female dependent scheme turned marriage into a material necessity for women. But for highly employable women, marriage becomes economically optional. Thus, the previously strong motivational and survival forces of economic need no longer promote marriage among today's highly employable women. So the incidence of the marriage meme, and especially the early marriage meme, has dropped.

Nevertheless, a more driven pursuit of marriage by less employable women could add another lasting replication force for the domestic woman meme. As discussed earlier, marriage greatly boosts a couple's willingness to reproduce. If a domestic calling motivates women to marry without giving them a disadvantage with money-conscious men, the net effect will be a higher marriage rate for home-oriented women. Therefore, the "domestic female" adherents can have an enhanced fertility rate due to a higher marriage rate. This makes one more propagation point preventing the domestic wife role from nearing extinction in modern economies.

CHORES

Gender roles also divide the household chores. Sewing, cooking, and laundry, for instance, usually go to females while maintenance and household repairs go to males. Such mores usually propagate as gender-based chore assignments in childhood. The belief that some essential chores are "manly" and others are "womanly" can stem partly from other sex stereotypes and partly from a replication advantage peculiar to the chore memes. The memes create impediments to living without members of the opposite sex, making hosts uneasy about staying single long into adulthood. Moving out of the parents' house involves either finding a mate, accepting slightly stigmatized chores, paying for hired help, or letting important chores go undone. Such alternatives raise the young adult's priority for finding a mate. That, in turn, can lead them to begin their reproductive careers earlier, which usually produces more numerous offspring. It also accelerates replication by shortening the time between generations.

RESPONSIBILITY AND HELPLESSNESS

Women's and men's family roles derive partly from their respective mating roles, and mating roles partly derive from family roles. Roles played in courtship extend throughout marriage and parenthood, where they help define family gender roles. Prominent examples—closely related to the traditional gender work roles—are the personality memes of "girlish helplessness" and "manly responsibility."

"Girlish helplessness" refers to a personality image women can display toward men, from courtship through marriage. It consists in various degrees of several behaviors: a woman pretending to be less intelligent than her man or her true self, avoiding date expenses, shunning responsibility for daily contact or transportation, acting whimsically, identifying as a "girl" during womanhood, taking on airs of innocence, relating deferentially, and so forth.

"Manly responsibility" refers to an essentially complementary role: trying to act "smart," calmly assuming expenses, accepting responsibility for daily contact and transportation, exhibiting dependable conduct, identifying as a man not a boy, assuming airs of worldliness, relating assertively, and so forth.

These learned personality images could, of course, be labeled in a gender-neutral manner as "youthful helplessness" and "grown-up responsibility." The real question is why they evolved to be so widely imparted on the basis of *gender*, starting in childhood. Why did "youthful helplessness" become more widespread among women and "grown-up responsibil-ity" more widespread among men as personality traits? Indeed, why did they even become integrated into many people's senses of gender identity?

All "girlishly helpless" behaviors mimic somewhat the intrinsic "personality" of any young child (boy or girl). Young children have less mental aptitude, cannot pay bills, take little responsibility for contact with others or mutual transportation, behave whimsically, are deemed "innocent" by adults, and are preferred to relate deferentially to adults. Therefore, a woman who projects a "helpless" image toward a man tests his reaction to a child—without needing any conscious or subconscious plan. If the man accepts this childlike, innocent helplessness and responds with "manly responsibility," he shows more promise for acting that way as a father with real children. He also shows promise for supporting a wife slowed down by pregnancy or nursing. In short, he makes a more plausible fam-ily man. The "girlish helplessness" meme acts as a "family man finder" for its female host, thereby explaining its replication advantage. Whether a woman deliberately seeks a family man or not, mating with one usually boosts her reproductive career. This of course gets her meme imitated by more young girls than happens with a "womanly responsibility" role. The "help-less" meme thus enjoys a gender-linked version of parental propagation.

This meme acts *blindly,* in that it has no built-in sensitiv-ity to what individual women want, and presumes no uniform desire for children among its hosts. Thus, *blindly,* it finds family men even for women who plan to remain childless. This in turn helps some of them change their mind later and have children, ultimately passing down more copies of the "girlish helpless-ness" meme.

The mate-screening action of "girlish helplessness" is actually twofold: first, it wards off courtly overtures from men who do not wish to assume responsibility for helpless others. Second, it provides female hosts with a basis for rejecting those men who respond with "inadequate" levels of "manly responsibility," even if they don't shun "girlish helplessness." Thus, a meme explicitly or implicitly specifying the rejection of such men can copropagate with the "girlish helplessness" meme. Consider a woman whose meme construes "manly responsibility" reactions to "girlish helplessness" as "treating her like a woman." The host may then take a suitor's failure to "treat her like a woman" as a violation of her gender identity, an event that precludes further courtship. This rejective mate-screening mechanism can strengthen the family-man-finding action of "girlish helplessness." The meme's close link to gender identity can partly explain why girlish helplessness and manly responsibility are often viewed as gender traits and not mere traditions.

The rejection mechanism works secondarily as a memetic preservation mechanism. When memes lead women to cancel courtship with a man of insufficient manly responsibility, the memes thereby prevent him from influencing her to discard the "helpless" role identity, and all the memes supporting it. Any indignation she feels from her memes' imputing gender violation further shuts off communication between them. By thus preventing hosts of helpless role identities from becoming non-hosts, the rejection mechanism helps sustain the role's prevalence.

The evolution of "family-man finder" memes among women promotes coevolution of the required fatherly response among males. With a "fatherly responsibility" response widely required by women, the men who give the response enjoy more mating success and parental meme transmission. This gives a reproductive edge to the manly responsibility meme.

Behavioral reinforcement also spreads manly responsibility in courtship wherever women prefer it. When men happen to give this role response to girlish helplessness, they are more often rewarded by the female population. This reinforcement selectively increases the frequency and persistence of manly responsibility behaviors in individual men. Their cognitive role identity can then easily follow their established behavior patterns.

Strongly motivated cognition can also help men to figure out what women expect of them, and act accordingly. Observing and copying successfully mating men play a big part here. It's thought contagion by example display, combining aspects of proselytic, motivational, and cognitive transmission. Listening to others give courtship advice can transmit the memes even more directly. Once the male population has widely adopted its mating role identity, that role reinforces women's role identity through similar conditioning, cognition, and peer imitation.

In some cases of manly responsibility, men show a false or exaggerated love for the helpless and dependent. This somewhat impairs the function of girlish helplessness as a test of men's child affinity, reducing its action as a true family-man finder. Natural selection could counter by favoring "improved versions" that require a more complete or deeply ingrained manly responsibility. Meanwhile, the occasional men who refrain from responsibility gestures—despite all advantages of compliance—may be exceptionally *averse* to helpless dependents. This could help maintain replication advantages for women to screen them out.

Astute readers may wonder why boyish helplessness doesn't become equally common as a family-woman finder for its male hosts.

Helplessness derives part of its gender linkage from compatibility with partner age preferences. As discussed in the next chapter, males evolved an average preference for younger mates while females evolved a preference for older mates. Helpless, childlike behavior can therefore help a woman attract a man more often than vice versa. This gives some added parental advantage to girlish helplessness over boyish helplessness.

Men may also achieve less replication gain from testing women's willingness to care for helpless dependents. Mammalian instincts usually give women a faster and stronger bond to offspring, and prevailing female culture reinforces the instincts. This permits men to forgo such elaborate testing of women's child care prospects.

Girlish helplessness also shows compatibility with the old-fashioned male breadwinner meme, whereas boyish helplessness precludes a male breadwinner system. So the forces that created the male breadwinner norm also gave girlish helplessness a big lead over boyish helplessness.

The replication forces that produced girlish helplessness substantially continue for modern well-employed women. Screening for the dependable breadwinners of domestic wives is outmoded as a replication advantage to career women. Yet the child affinity screening achieved by girlish helplessness becomes much more important in a modern economy. Modern contraceptives make fatherhood more easily avoidable for men who don't want it. And since few modern men desire children for their farm labor value, they hold less interest in fatherhood than did their grandfathers, and more inclination to see children as helpless dependents. These changes can actually *raise* the replication advantage for modern women who screen their suitors' reaction to helpless dependency.

Women's pursuit of high career goals while often keeping a "helpless" courtship role toughens the challenge of forming a nonsexist work force. The lingering meme of males as superior breadwinners creates some of the challenge. But when serious career women assume relatively childlike courtship roles, confusion can result among men. The confusion is greatest when women seek responsible leadership roles. Here they can either be denied the job, or have trouble being taken seriously after getting it. These problems can affect both women's jobless rate and their attitude toward employment. The traditional home-maker role may pick up some adherents from those suffering such effects, helping it maintain some prevalence in modern times.

In order for memetic courtship roles to replicate parentally, their influence must extend beyond courtship, into marriage. After behaving more helplessly in courtship, women often behave more deferentially in marriage. Men in turn behave more dominantly, assuming head-of-household status in many past and present families. Male breadwinner memes also strengthen men's historical authority role in the family. Both the courtship and the breadwinner roles can partially cause and result from male dominance memes, especially if male domi-nance has replication advantages of its own.

MALE DOMINANCE AND FEMALE SUBSERVIENCE

Female and male physical differences contribute cognitive and motivational acceptance to the male dominance meme, while working against the female dominance meme. The heavier, stronger partner has a physical advantage in dominating the smaller, weaker mate in a one-to-one contest. Yet greater phys-ical ability to dominate might not entirely explain the histori-cally prevalent belief that men *should* dominate. Indeed, our closest primate relative, the bonobo, has a social structure in which smaller, weaker females dominate bigger, stronger males. Their females simply gang up on any male who tries to domi-nate by force.

In humans, who have much less sex than bonobos, the tra-dition of male dominance may flourish parentally from its effects on sex. Giving a man authority in sexual matters allows him to have sex when *his* urge is greatest and to do it in ways he finds most stimulating. Increasing the likelihood of *his* arousal and orgasm increases the likelihood of *her* pregnancy. The woman may actually have less frequent orgasms from this arrangement, but the man's frequency of intravaginal orgasm affects fertility more than the woman's.

The idea that a woman's role is to please her husband can further ensure male arousal, but it can also increase the quantity of sex. According to the National Health and Social Life Survey, men think about sex more often than women do. So memes assigning women the duty of pleasing the more sex-minded mate should cause more sex, and hence, more children raised with female subservience memes.

Women's movements have reduced female subservience and male dominance memes in modern times, but centuries of parental replication helped these memes define the "traditional" family structures in most of the world.

PATRILINEAL NAMES

The tradition that women receive last names from their dominant husbands also replicates parentally. The practice pressures couples to have more children, on average, in order to pass down their family names into the next generation. Specifically, parents who as yet have all girls can feel motivated to "try again" in order to have a son. Of course, patrilineal versus matrilineal naming does not hinge on just this pressure. Taken alone, the two alternatives should fare equally well. But in the context of a male-dominated household, the replication advantage favors patrilineal naming. As head of household, the man can simply use his greater power to name the family after himself—a choice that most men favor motivationally. But as head of household, men also have greater say in whether to try for more children. So resting the family name with the key reproductive decision maker leads more often to the decision to have more children.

The patrilineal naming meme helps replicate the added idea that the family name *must* propagate into future generations—or that not doing so amounts to a kind of death. This meme derives its parental advantage, in turn, by enhancing reproduction for the patrilineal naming meme. The two memes thus replicate as a symbiotic combination.

PATRILINEAL INHERITANCE

Patrilineal wealth inheritance also emerges as a historically widespread practice.

Clearly, inheritance by children can help them have grandchildren. So a simple offspring inheritance meme self-replicates by causing more descendants for its hosts. Willing wealth to recipients other than descendants lacks that advantage, but may have proselytic strengths if recipients use the wealth to spread beliefs.

The patrilineal inheritance meme combines offspring inheritance with a provision that sons get inheritance priority over daughters. Historically, this meme enjoyed replication advantages from the greater effect of wealth on the mating success of sons than of daughters.

Wealth has traditionally set men's mating "eligibility" much more than women's. Indeed, the man who gave too much priority to finding a woman of great income or net worth would likely go unmated. Only the dowry could receive his serious priority in mating. Natural selection weeds out mating priorities that frequently leave hosts unmated, so women's "eligibility" depends slightly on their wealth and less on their income.

Since the man historically played a sole breadwinner role, his economic resources were the couple's primary means to safely having children. Women who gave priority to finding a man of means therefore stood to average more children by finding a secure setting for having them. Marrying a poor man could seriously reduce reproductive intent. Hence the growth of a large population of women who give high priority to a suitor's wealth.

These financial "eligibility" memes cause sons to receive more mating boost per unit inheritance than daughters receive. Additionally, more women than men pass their reproductive years by the time their parents die and leave an estate. Men generally pass their reproductive years when their partners reach menopause. But even this usually happens later for men because most men marry younger partners. So parents bequeathing their estates preferentially to sons tend to leave more grandchildren, due to both "eligibility" and biological clocks. The extra grandchildren give patrilineal inheritance its historical replication edge over egalitarian alternatives. Meanwhile, the reduced number of grandchildren with matrilineal inheritance explains the low historical prevalence of that arrangement.

Patrilineal inheritance intensifies the economic disparities between men and women. The disparity intensifies the replication loss to men who view wealth as a high mating priority, thereby reinforcing one of the evolutionary causes of patrilineal inheritance.

The replication advantages of inheritance memes are sensitive to changes in host life expectancy. The longer a couple lives into their children's adulthood, the less difference their estate can make in promoting grandchildren. In the days when patrilineal inheritance evolved, life expectancies were short enough for typical children to inherit estates while young enough to spend on reproduction. Today's life expectancies are long enough to delay inheritance beyond the heir's reproductive years. So patrilineal inheritance now enjoys less replication advantage over competing schemes; even offspring inheritance has less replication advantage over its alternatives.

REVISING THE ROLES

Proselytically spreading beliefs undo many role standards that evolved by parental replication. Women who believe that sex-based employment, chore, authority, naming, and inheritance roles are unfair often speak up to better their own and each other's situation. The prior growth of egalitarian thought probably lent some cognitive receptivity to the women's movement in many countries. Meanwhile, increasing population density, more leisure time, easy transportation, and fast communication all boost the proselytic rates of modern times. Average hosts of revised gender roles thus reach more nonhosts per year in modern times than in centuries past. This helps women's liberation ideas achieve the critical self-sustaining growth rate of more than one transmission per host per lifetime.

Women's entry into the work force also gives them more power to refuse traditional roles in other settings. A woman can simply live without a "man of the house" if he doesn't share her revised role concepts. This, of course, gives new motives for men to accept the changing roles.

Financial independence also gives women more power to leave sexually unsatisfying relationships. This motivates men to play their sexual dominance and mating initiator roles with greater attention to their partners' satisfaction. The rise of proselytically spreading sexual memes also plays a part, as discussed in the next chapter.

SYMBIOTIC MEMES

Each meme defining family structure must share its host with other such memes. Yet the memes of single parenthood, for instance, replicate poorly when combined with "girlish helplessness." Such mutually antagonistic memes tend to go extinct as a combination even while they thrive and multiply in separate populations. Natural selection favors the growth of symbiotic meme sets, but fails to give us a universal family structure that can forever win the population race.

OPTIMISM

One meme compatible with nearly all family structures is optimism. People generally maintain a slightly more optimistic outlook than reality warrants, because the optimistic personality meme survives and passes down through the generations more prevalently than do realism and pessimism. Part of this comes about from self-fulfilling outlooks, as optimism effects a better future than does pessimism. Without it, people miss their goals by giving up in cases where perseverance pays. Yet optimism also replicates by encouraging the usually daring decision to begin a family and have more children. Because of its great expense, willfully embarking on child raising requires an optimistic view of one's future. Optimists have children under circumstances where pessimists refrain, therefore passing down their outlook in greater proportions. So as future family structures remain unclear, the future of optimism looks bright.

4

SEXUALLY
TRANSMITTED BELIEF:
THE CLASH OF FREEDOM
AND RESTRICTION

Ideas have to be wedded to action;
if there is no sex, no vitality in them,
there is no action.
—HENRY MILLER

Conflicting evolutionary forces make sex and mating a volatile spot in the ideosphere. Memes restricting sex and mating typically spread by permeating and expanding the family network. Yet sexual pleasures generate strong proselytic drives, sometimes supporting and sometimes opposing parental replication.

EXTRAMARITAL SEX

The most basic sexual norms concern whether to have sex or not. Within marriage, most evolutionary forces line up in favor of having it. Outside marriage, the evolutionary conflicts arise. Here the premarital sex taboos compete with consenting adult liberties, and both sides have major replication advantages.

Paradoxically, the taboo against premarital sex gains some replication advantage parentally, at least in biparental cultures. While reducing premarital reproduction, the taboo still raises its adherents' total reproduction. By giving sexual incentive to marriage, it persuades hosts either to marry or to marry younger. As noted earlier, marriage makes couples feel more secure about each other's intentions to raise children jointly, thus increasing their willingness to procreate. So the meme that motivates marriage usually increases adherents' lifetime fertility.

Motivating earlier marriage adds to the effect. The sooner people get married, the more time they spend in the reproductively "safe" setting it affords. The extra children resulting from faster and more certain marriage can easily make up for the premarital births "lost" by shunning premarital sex.

Those welcoming premarital sex usually start their sexual careers sooner, but often with more attention to birth control. The old-fashioned options of early withdrawal and nonvaginal sex, along with modern birth control options, make sex without parenthood feasible. And by staying unmarried longer, they have their childless plans remaining in effect longer. That reduces the number of children they end up having, leaving the reproductive edge to those holding the taboo.

More importantly, the same kin persuasion forces that helped create marriage also propagate the premarital sex taboo. Family economics motivates people to stop kin—especially females—from reproducing before securing a partner's promise of marital support. So hosts of the premarital sex taboo emphatically retransmit it to their children and other close relatives.

Modern birth control reduces the motive for such kin persuasion in recent decades, allowing premarital sex taboos to recede. Sexually motivated proselytism also changes the picture, sometimes putting the premarital sex taboo into steep decline. People who believe in having premarital sex can have sex before, during, and after marriage, provided they have a consenting partner. The need for partner agreement motivates them to sexually liberalize any dating partners still opposed to premarital sex. Taboo hosts, on the other hand, typically feel little sexual incentive for spreading their beliefs widely. So the permissive meme better harnesses erotic motives toward proselytism.

Many other factors tip the balance in different times and places. Birth control, diseases, religions, and government all play a part. Urbanization, communications, transportation, leisure time, and other proselytic accelerants can favor the permissive side, but can also help spread conservative religions. Finally, the modern media ensure wide exposure to both competing memes. Yet the most consistent and lasting replication forces affecting premarital sex remain amorous proselytism, birth rates, child raising, and kin persuasion.

CHASTITY

The belief that chastity is precious relates closely to the premarital sex taboo. Ideas that sex is either unnecessary, distasteful, or a necessary evil are all variants of the chastity meme.

Memes exalting chastity and devaluing sex would seem parentally doomed. Yet just the opposite is true. The gender biases in promarriage kin persuasion can set up a population where women value marriage more than men do and men value freedom more than women do. This makes the exchange of vows feel like an unfair trade. The commitment given is more highly prized by women while the freedom sacrificed is more highly prized by men. This condition where men see marriage as shortchanging them fosters prochastity memes in women. When women memetically value chastity more than men do, it follows that men value sex more than women do. This facilitates an unspoken barter that can feel more fair than a simple exchange of vows alone. Men give up their valued freedom, while women give up their valued chastity. Meanwhile women gain commitment, while men gain sex. So the memetic valuation of chastity by women spreads parentally by securing a higher rate of marriage for its female hosts.

The idea that women should appear uninterested in sex works much like the explicit chastity meme. It no longer suggests that women relinquish something in symmetry with the prized freedom that men relinquish. But it does suggest that men receive something they value more, sex, while women receive something they value more, commitment. Perhaps this forms part of the unconscious logic behind the idea that sex "consummates" marriage, though more serious reasons also apply.

The match between women's and men's *biological* sex drive may actually be closer than cultural norms suggest, especially considering women's multiple orgasm potential. Yet appearing uninterested in sex may often prevent women from realizing that potential. When men get the idea that women aren't very interested in sex, they may give less attention to pleasing their partners. So the chastity meme and its close relatives can contribute to the sexual dissatisfaction voiced by women in recent decades. Other memetic reasons behind these "sexual inequity" issues arise later.

"Precious chastity" and related memes function symbiotically with the premarital sex taboo, since valuing chastity supports obedience to the premarital sex taboo. Parents and relatives therefore advocate "precious chastity" as a way of bolstering premarital sex taboos, helping chastity spread by kin persuasion. Together, the memes give their hosts a net marriage incentive and a hard stance in bargaining for the partner's marriage vows. The marriage, in turn, launches reproductive careers and transmits the values into more children.

Much sexually motivated proselytism goes to dissuade women from chastity memes, contributing to chastity's declining valuation in modern times. The subtler alternative of feigning a low female sex drive may better resist such proselytism. Weak sex drives, after all, hardly appear changeable through persuasion. So men probably try less often, thereby selectively preserving sexual indifference memes over chastity-valuing memes.

PROMISCUITY

Sexually motivated proselytism certainly goes beyond the subjects of chastity and premarital sex, as in the spread of sexual promiscuity memes. Whether driven by lust or status, those who believe in having a "crowded" sex life often hold the proselytic advantage over monogamists. True, both sexual monogamists and "pluralists" may wish to spread their memes to anyone they find attractive. Yet monogamists tend to stop this attraction-motivated proselytism after they find their one sexual relationship. Meanwhile, pluralists continue proselytizing potential partners even after starting one or more sexual relationships. Their messages can also reach social bystanders, helping ideas jump from man to man or woman to woman rather than just man to woman to man.

People also retransmit the promiscuity meme just by living promiscuously enough for nonpromiscuous partners to find out about it, as they often do. Those finding out can then feel pressured either to cancel the relationship or to restore balance by taking multiple partners themselves. This tends to expose the newest partners to promiscuity memes as well, continuing the cycle.

So promiscuity memes enjoy episodes of intense proselytic replication. Their propagation advantages fed the explosive growth of free sex that distinguished the era known as the "sexual revolution."

As often happens, conversions subside when most persuadable people have converted. Promiscuity apparently reached this level during its latest upsurge. That left its short-term fate up to the preservational mode, where it seems to face a net disadvantage. Those tired of loose bonds and perpetual efforts at landing new mates eventually dropped out of the promiscuity set, as did those who felt that their real desires were not being met. This started a first phase of decline in modern American promiscuity.

Sexually transmitted beliefs such as the promiscuity meme prime their host populations for analogously transmitted diseases. Once an (STD) epidemic happens, both the motivational and proselytic stories change for the promiscuity meme. Hosts develop health motives for converting to the monogamy meme, and then for spreading it to potential or actual sex partners. Health-motivated monogamy memes stormed the population during the herpes scare, and greatly intensified with the chilling news of AIDS. The AIDS epidemic created an added proselytic drive for monogamy: the desire to spread the meme to save lives among friends and loved ones who weren't even prospective sex partners. Of course, promiscuity memes lost some prevalence when hosts died of the disease itself. Yet hundreds of times more people converted away from promiscuity memes to proselytically spreading "safety-through-monogamy" memes. These conversions will bring down STD rates, possibly to the point where future generations can grow up with little direct experience of them. That would then set the stage for a new sexual revolution and perhaps even a new disease to help end it.

Conflicting evolutionary forces produce fluctuating norms in matters of *who* is an eligible mate, as well as how many mates one may have. Such norms affect whether an eligible mate may be rich or poor, young or old, same-sex or opposite-sex, et cetera.

HOMOSEXUALITY

Not surprisingly, evolution made the eligibility memes fierce in matters of homosexual versus heterosexual mating. These memes may interact so strongly with genetic evolution that the fates of the memes and the genes cannot be totally separated. The biological factors affecting sexual preference apparently include genes affecting brain development. Such genes might, for example, influence the recently discovered section of hippocampus related to sexual orientation. The prenatal hormone environment can also play a part, giving a role to maternal genes. Even something as simple as long eyelashes on men might appeal more to other men than to women—sending the bisexually capable toward homosexual lives. Still other genetic and environmental factors may also play major parts, awaiting further scientific discovery.

One can easily imagine that genes favoring homosexuality would go extinct prehistorically, for lack of reproduction. Yet at very low prevalence, homosexually inclined people would have found it virtually impossible to find a homosexual mate, pressuring them to try heterosexual mating to whatever extent they could. Their actions would resemble the way incarcerated heterosexual men often choose the nearest alternative to women. So their genes may have replicated at almost the rate of innate heterosexuals' genes, letting homosexually inclining genes hold a persistent low prevalence rate. A similar mechanism prevents recessive genes from going fully extinct.

So long as genetic factors for homosexuality avoided extinction, the taboo against homosexuality was parentally transmitted more than tolerant memes. Taboo hosts and non-hosts may have experienced the same frequency of homosexual drives, but the taboo urged hosts to suppress these feelings. This promoted heterosexual mating by making celibacy the only "legitimate" alternative. So homosexually inclined but memetically restrained people usually found heterosexual relationships if they had any heterosexual capacity at all. Meanwhile, taboo-free homosexuals sought fewer heterosexual and more homosexual relationships. So taboo-free homosexuals had fewer children than those holding the taboo. The same would apply with even greater force for bisexuality, which allows for simpler compliance with a ban on same-sex relationships. The taboo's host population thus held a parental replication edge over the nontaboo population. Compounding with each generation over hundreds of generations, the replication difference fueled much of the taboo's growth from its first few hosts to its current billions.

After expanding parentally, the taboo added proselytism and adversative effects to its replication profile. Today's adherents eagerly express taboo conformity by denouncing homosexuality, especially if they suspect that other hosts are listening. Doing so guards against ostracism and harassment by the taboo-holding crowd. Not surprisingly, it happens most among those worried about their own images, such as young males and people without opposite sex partners. The declarations incidentally spread the taboo to listening nonhosts as well. On hearing the message, heterosexual nonadherents can see social safety to gain and little to lose by also adopting the taboo and expressing it.

As insecurities arising from the homosexuality taboo feed

on themselves, hosts often go well beyond vocal expressions. Those seeking to distance themselves from suspicion and self-suspicion can turn to violence, persecution, discrimination, and ostracism against both gays and those holding tolerant opinions. By intimidating others into silence, the intolerant block the spread of competing views, enhancing the competitive advantage of intolerant memes.

Homosexuals can also adopt the taboo, often long before sexual maturity. They either obey the taboo or suffer anxiety and guilt by secretly breaking it. Still other homosexuals falsely profess taboo adherence to project the heterosexual images demanded by real adherents. Like the heterosexual taboo hosts, they all communicate the taboo, furthering its proselytic transmission.

Among its growing host population, the taboo induces many with innately homosexual orientations to settle for heterosexual lives even when they can find homosexual mates. By restoring fertility for genes favoring homosexuality, the homosexuality taboo ironically makes the genes' incidence start rising. After many generations, "homosexual genotypes" can increment from rarity to commonality. They still wouldn't surpass "heterosexual genotypes," just expand enough for homosexually inclined people to meet frequently while maintaining totally heterosexual life-styles.

Now every taboo has its dropouts and its unpersuadables. Such unbelievers in the homosexuality taboo include those with genetically homosexual drives. Yet before a visible and accessible movement emerged, gays who adopted progay ideas still felt isolated from each other and hence, unable to mate easily. Desires for satisfying relationships motivated many of these people to share their accepting views of homosexuality with anyone they regarded as a "closeted" potential mate.

Occasionally gays succeeded at quietly spreading moral acceptance of homosexuality to a closeted homosexual. During times of low genetic prevalence, the occasion would have been rare. Gay to gay conversions would have fizzled out at less than a self-sustaining rate. Too many of those exposed to the message would have been heterosexuals with little motivation to adopt it and even less motivation to retransmit it.

But as genetically gay inclinations rose due to taboo adherence, more people felt motivated to independently adopt the belief that "Homosexuality is morally legitimate." Personal motives for spreading the word to others also became more common. But until recently, the culture of intolerance repressed most speech for the moral legitimacy meme. Motives such as relating socially, helping family, taking political action, and pursuing intellectual expression seldom justified the severe risks of expressing progay thoughts. Yet amorous motives were often strong enough to outweigh the risks. And as homosexually amorous motives proliferated genetically, the moral legitimacy meme achieved self-sustained propagation under repressive conditions: morally self-accepting gays went from converting few latently gay taboo adherents to converting several per decade. The increasing urbanization, population density, leisure time, communications, and transportation that enhance all proselytism helped cross the threshold into self-sustained meme transmission. At this point, a rapidly propagating movement developed.

Once enough homosexually inclined people accepted the moral legitimacy meme, the movement took on a civil rights dimension. Many actively gay people felt practical motives to persuade others to tolerate gay relationships. Legalizing homosexual sex, stopping hate crimes, and retaining employment, housing, and social participation replaced gaining access to mates as leading motives for meme transmission. The public discussion of homosexuality incidentally gave latent gays a new source of exposure to moral legitimacy beliefs, widely supplanting amorous persuasion as a way of encountering progay beliefs.

As more people became aware of homosexuality, they also heard about *closet* homosexuality, giving heterosexuals an element of doubt about prospective partners. Women in particular worried that the men they dated might someday reveal themselves as gay. To prove that they were *not* such "closet cases," heterosexual men who held gay-acceptance memes began openly expressing those thoughts when the subject came up—a way of indicating that if they *were* gay, they would have already lived accordingly. Though ironically similar to other men's motives for spreading *anti*gay memes, these newly sophisticated meme transmissions still favor growing acceptance of homosexuality.

If, however, the movement lets most homosexually inclined people live homosexual lives, their average fertility rate comes thundering down to a low level. This reduced gene transmission leaves the next generation sparsely populated with innately homosexual inclinations. Progay beliefs replicate less proselytically at that point, since a diminishing fraction of listeners have personal or familial motives for adopting and retransmitting the memes. As the meme's proselytic rate drops below its self-sustaining rate, the movement dwindles, especially when the life span of prior adherents has passed.

The population returns to its earlier state of scarce "homosexuality genes," scarce gay legitimacy memes, and widespread taboo memes. So those few with homosexually inclining genes again feign heterosexuality, starting the cycle all over again with a gradually rising gene prevalence. Because so many factors complicate the picture, the whole cycle should fluctuate in both amplitude and timing.

Throughout the process, other memes can deter their hosts from homosexual behavior, replicating much as the outright taboo does. For instance, the belief that male homosexuality requires anal sex deters homosexual mating in those male hosts who dread anal sex. The idea thereby enhances its hosts' fertility rates wherever the moral taboo alone seems uncompelling. The widespread meme also ensures that most males who do adopt homosexual life-styles will be those who tacitly accept the possibility of anal sex. Some homosexually inclined hosts who shun anal sex may do so by continuing to act heterosexually. So the "anal homosexuality" meme can become a self-fulfilling belief once it spreads parentally. A secondary issue in the epidemiology of taboos, it plays a larger role for human immunodeficiency virus (HIV), as discussed later.

GAY GENDER DIFFERENCES

Active communities of lesbians and gay males differ in matters such as their sheer numbers and the incidence of promiscuous sex, and some of the differences arise memetically.

With sex segregation present, motives for spreading the promiscuity meme work differently among homosexual people than in the heterosexual case discussed earlier. Since female culture values monogamy more than male culture does, one would expect less promiscuity in lesbians than gay men. Moreover, memetic and genetic forces lead the male population to frequently assume an approach role in mating, turning more men into sexually motivated proselytists. When one gay man spreads a promiscuity meme to another, the new host, being male, often takes new initiatives at retransmitting the meme to potential partners. This strengthens the recursive aspect for the meme in gay men. So male approach-role memes that replicate heterosexually carry over to give homosexual males a higher incidence of promiscuity memes than seen among homosexual females.

Since gay legitimacy memes can also spread by sexually

motivated proselytism, the higher rate of male proselytism spreads the memes more vigorously in gay men than in lesbians. The women, on the other hand, probably receive more assertive sexual "recruitment" from heterosexual men than from lesbians. Men can usually offer women more wealth, too. These factors help homosexual living propagate more among men than among women.

Actively proselytizing men also try harder with attractive partners, so one expects disproportionate fractions of both attractive men living homosexual lives and attractive women living heterosexual lives. After the effect causes selective depletion, *remaining* populations of actively heterosexual men and homosexual women should contain proportionately fewer attractive people—at least to *men's* eyes.

BREAST FETISHES

Homosexuality and its taboo affect the "fashionability" of certain sexual fetishes in heterosexual males. Specifically, a "mandatory breast fetish" meme evolves and spreads, while other fetishes receive less emphasis. The memes deflect attraction-related behaviors from the course that biological forces alone would promote.

The role of homosexuality and its taboo in heterosexual fetish memes starts during youth. By voicing attraction to protruding breasts, males can publicly imply their exclusive heterosexuality—because protruding breasts are only noticed publicly on females. Although hips much wider than waist are also distinctively female, they make subtler candidates for fetish fashion statements and take more words to describe. Both sexes have legs and posteriors, but with mainly qualitative differences. Declaring inherent heterosexuality through "attraction" to these other body parts is much more difficult, especially in early adolescence. Indeed, young males may feel inhibited from discussing female posteriors because it reminds them of anal sex and homosexuality, subjects they wish to publicly shun. So protruding breasts get disproportionate "air time" in male sex talk.

As homophobic peers make boys concerned with projecting the "solidly heterosexual" image, their fear of suspicion gives proselytic impetus to the breast fetish identity meme. Collective schooling, dense populations, and leisure time all boost the proselytic effect in modern times. The host may actually lack strong attraction to breasts, but still adopt the public identity and even the self-identity of having that fetish. The more prevalent the meme becomes, the more outnumbered and "abnormal" nonhosts feel, increasing the pressure on them to convert. The conversions apparently climax during adolescence and early adulthood, when sexual identity posturing reaches its peak. These memes of youth often go on to shape mating choices well into adulthood.

So memetic breast fetishes have shaped the progression of American male culture toward greater obsession with bigger breasts. In much of Europe, where males hold less fear of latent homosexuality, the culture places less emphasis on large breasts.

FAT AND THIN

Even as men evolved preferences for large busts, they also evolved preferences for trimmer dimensions elsewhere on women's bodies, again suggesting a meme at work.

One conventional explanation for men's change of weight preference is the changing value of body fat as a class indicator. Corpulence indicated high economic status back when most people struggled to find steady food. But as societies developed, most citizens enjoyed securely abundant food, rendering obesity obsolete as a status indicator. Moreover, thinness could rise in status because of its increased scarcity and because it indicated recreations more expensive than eating.

That explanation, however, fails to tell why the evolving fat and thin preferences applied mostly to women, even when men's social status mattered more than women's in mating. Memetics rounds out the explanation with fertility considerations that apply specifically to the shape of women.

Biology safeguards pregnancies and newborns by linking women's body fat to fertility. Women need a certain proportion of body fat to start and continue ovulation. Men who preferred fatter women therefore fathered more children in centuries past, allowing them to outpopulate men with lean partner preferences. Men who preferred even more fat than needed for ovulation enjoyed still more reproductive success due to better protection against famine.

The reproductive value of body fat diminishes in modern societies, where the food supply is so abundant and fatty that women rarely fall below the body-fat threshold for ovulation. Moreover, widespread famine never threatens pregnant or nursing women in modern rich countries. The replication advantages for men who prefer corpulent women therefore vanish as well.

Besides losing its old disadvantage, the lean-partner preference achieves a new replication advantage in richly fed countries. Eating abundant high-fat food causes people to gain weight as they age. So women's body-fat percentage now correlates with their age. But men who prefer young women can lead longer reproductive careers, replicating their memes into more sons. By thus favoring young women, the lean-partner preference out replicates the fat-partner preference in modern, well-fed societies.

Weight preferences applying more to women than to men also follow from men's greater propensity to choose partners by physical attractiveness. As noted in the last chapter, memes specifically favoring men's sexual arousal induce more reproduction than those favoring female arousal. So the idea of choosing partners by physical attractiveness replicates as a male meme more than as a female meme. Yet women generally emphasize partner wealth more than men do, lowering the priority they can give to a mate's physique.

MATING BY CLASS

On the subject of class-minded mating by women, sociobiology offers an explanation based on genetic fitness—specifically, a reproductive advantage to women who prefer wealthy mates. Partner wealth would matter especially to women because a female cannot have as many offspring as a male can; so women must secure good investment in each child's survival and reproduction.

Purely memetic arguments can also explain class-minded mating by women. At the very least, the reproductive advantage of having a wealthy mate can parentally propagate a woman's *memes* as well as her genes.

Kin persuasion also replicates women's partner wealth standards. A girl's parents and other relatives in traditional settings know that her socioeconomic future depends mainly on how "well" she marries. They can therefore tell her to marry well for her own good. Moreover, if she and her children face economic hardships, she may need the help of parents and siblings, giving close kin a purely selfish reason for imparting lucrative marriage memes.

The "marry money" meme also propagates disproportionately upward, concentrating with each ascending socioeconomic stratum. It affects women most intensely because women's status still depends largely on their husbands' status. The higher the stratum, the higher the proportion of women who got there or stayed there by screening suitors for wealth. Meanwhile, women with mild or indifferent mate-wealth preferences should more often marry into lower wealth brackets. As memes replicate into successive generations of daughters, even the middle class fills up with women who set partner wealth standards. So memetics alone can sufficiently explain partner wealth preference.

SEX, AGE, AND CLASS REBELLION

Like most restrictive mating memes, women's wealth preferences inspire men to express alternative memes. Amorous men of modest resources spread the idea of temporarily suspending women's class requirements. They often combine this message with forecasts of upward mobility, especially during the optimism of youth. And in youth, many women feel free to wait for their socioeconomic "Mr. Rights." The idea of *avoiding* young marriage spreads synergistically by assuring women's right to eventually mate by class. This gives young populations looser norms for both marriage and class. The surge of baby boomers into adolescence and early adulthood thus provides one reason for the widely relaxed class and marriage memes of the 1960s and 1970s.

The baby boom also affected class mating by varying the sexual balance of power. With men choosing younger women, and vice versa, the rising phase of the baby boom produced a surplus of younger women per older man. Each man born in 1950 could choose among 1.1 women born in 1953. After pairing off 80 percent of the men, the small difference in sex ratio expands palpably to a 3 women per 2 men margin. That forced many women to compete by compromising on class, commitment, and other matters, while men imparted their memes with greater power. Thus, the rising-phase baby boomers led the "sexual revolution."

The situation reverses for declining-phase baby boomers, leaving up to 3 men per 2 women in unpaired groups. Empowered by their short supply, women could better assert and spread their memes on class and commitment. So declining-phase baby boomers entered a more class-minded and sexually conservative youth than their older counterparts.

Moreover, as male baby boomers aged, the most successful of them shifted their amorous proselytism in favor of mating by class. Suddenly favored by women's rich taste in men, they stopped speaking against it and gradually endorsed it. Likewise with female sexual freedom, which gave men opportunities when young but later threatened their established relationships. So the aging baby boomers countered the sexual revolution they had once fomented.

After choosing partners, people eventually decide what sex acts they will or will not perform. Here, the fertility differentials beget sexual conduct memes.

MASTURBATION

The masturbation taboo earlier illustrated quantity parental replication. Taboo adherents have fewer "acceptable" erotic alternatives, pressuring them toward more frequent vaginal sex. For singles, the taboo heightens the incentive to mate. Even those hosts who continue masturbating still want to find their partners quickly in order to reduce their guilt. For couples, the taboo may reduce both solitary and mutual masturbation, including any done for birth control. Male hosts can also produce higher sperm counts during intercourse by reducing their nonvaginal orgasms. All these effects tend to increase fertility rates for those holding the taboo.

Once the masturbation taboo outpopulates more permissive ideas, proselytism boosts the taboo further. Hosts become eager to "prove" their conformity to the taboo, especially if they suspect that other hosts are listening. Yet they can't prove their conformity to the taboo directly, so they often "demonstrate" an ideological incapacity to violate it. That usually means

expressing the taboo in the fiercest language possible or implying strict conformity by referring to masturbation in the context of insults. Such proselytism resembles what happens for
advanced transmission antigay memes.

On the other hand, most people who accept masturbation
see few reasons to proselytize, especially for solitary masturbation. Discussing the subject can suggest sexual frustration,
implying low status to listeners. Besides, those accepting solitary
masturbation feel little or even negative sex motive to persuade
others, since converts might become less available for partnered
sex. That leaves few advocates of autoeroticism outside its modern consideration in sex research and disease control.

Masturbation taboos have declined somewhat in recent
years, with much of the change inspired by mass media. Indeed,
the very status as taboo makes masturbation and other sex topics prime material for commercial use: mention over the air-
waves can make people pay attention long enough to hear a
commercial, and then improve recall of the commercial by
"downloading" it to an aroused audience. The process incidentally conveys the idea that masturbation is normal and acceptable. Although the taboo remains widely entrenched, media
exposure over a few decades has caused a prevalence drop that
would previously have taken generations.

BIRTH CONTROL

Like masturbation, interrupted intercourse is one of the oldest
forms of birth control. People who reject the practice have
therefore outreplicated those who accept it, especially in the
days when parents controlled their children's meme sets closely.
The memes against birth control, including interrupted intercourse, offer the clearest examples of the quantity parental
effect. By raising extra babies, followers of these memes can
outpopulate nonhosts across various times and places.

The oldest birth control taboos, along with religious beliefs in fruitfully multiplying, suggest that sex exists solely for procreation. Indeed, the belief that God created sex solely for procreation works as an all-purpose birth control taboo. When new birth control technologies arrive, adherents of the all-purpose taboo continue with high fertility rates while others cut back. The reproductive difference expands, adding more advantage to the taboo—at least parentally.

In parts of the world with less advanced urbanization, communication, education, and transportation, parents remain a very strong source of people's morality. That pattern gives birth control taboos a special strength in developing countries.

Yet people do find reasons other than procreation for having sex. To most, accepting birth control promises to increase their sex lives. Those who accept birth control must proselytize if they desire nonprocreational sex with a taboo adherent. Married people who detest abstinence try to persuade spouses to accept birth control for economic or practical reasons. Yet sex alone often motivates proselytism for birth control, since sex often hinges on preventing pregnancies deemed unaffordable or illegitimate. Proselytic and motivational advantages overpower the taboo's parental replication in many societies—especially where urbanization, communications, and transportation facilitate the exchange of beliefs.

Kin persuasion further spreads the acceptance of birth control for reasons ironically similar to those discussed earlier for premarital celibacy. People feel strong economic motives to dissuade their offspring, siblings, and other relatives from unplanned or badly planned parenthood. Knowing the challenge of trying to preach sexual abstinence, they often regard condoms and pills as an easier sell—especially where the young can get the products easily. By combining lateral and vertical family transmission, the pro–birth control idea can thus offset much of its quantity parental handicap.

HOW TO DO IT

Memes specifying vaginal intercourse for all sex also gain moral prevalence by making adherents have children. Memes directly forbidding oral and anal intercourse increase the reproductive advantage still more by eliminating shades of doubt about how to act. Such meme sets join the birth control taboos among the most basic of parentally replicating ideas. Still, as with birth control, memes defending oral and anal sex still spread by sexually motivated persuasion, especially in modern countries.

Memes placing the man on top during intercourse can also boost fertility by giving men more control of the rhythm and pace. That, in turn, helps the man pursue his own climax, increasing the odds of pregnancy. Moreover, with the man on top, semen has a downward instead of upward path into the cervix. If it helps semen get there and stay there, then more pregnancies and meme replications should follow. Yet once again, sexuality motivates people to spread more permissive memes that allow women on top. The man-on-top memes spread, but not to universality.

SEX TALK

The taboo against *discussing* sex can propagate by helping preserve sexual conduct memes. As noted earlier, many parentally advantaged memes face stiff proselytic competition from sexual freedom memes. So refusing to talk about sex reduces the chance of receiving sexually motivated proselytism. For example, those who reject sex talk have less chance that prospective mates will persuade them to accept birth control. So more of them retain the high-fertility meme long enough to act on it by raising extra children. By preserving memes other than itself, the "don't talk about sex" meme wins its parental advantage indirectly.

This mechanism tends to produce a more prevalent and intense sex-talk taboo among women. Men usually act as initiators in sex and mating advances. So women are more likely than men to be the targets of sexually motivated proselytism. Thus, blocking the proselytism with a taboo affords a greater fertility difference to women than men.

Sex talk also provides a way for men to talk women out of class-minded mating strategies. Women who memetically restrict sex talk can therefore retain their class-minded mating memes long enough to apply them. When high proportions of class-mating women carry sex-talk restrictions, the restrictions become increasingly prevalent in ascending classes of women. Of course, unrestricted sex talk can also suggest that a woman is "easy," an impression that again interferes with class-minded mating.

The sex-talk taboo runs strong around young children, too. This is because the sex talk might *preempt* the transmission of parentally prolific memes rather than just risking a dropout. Here the taboo confers not just the preservation, but also the efficient *transmission* of quantity parental memes.

Since talking about talking about sex feels much like directly talking about sex, the sex-talk taboo can also enjoy a preservational advantage. Nonhosts have trouble trying to talk a host into dropping the meme if the host senses a taboo violation just by talking about talk. So besides preserving family-expanding sex taboos, the "don't talk about sex" meme preserves *itself* within its adherents' minds.

An indicator of its historical force, the taboo against sex talk apparently affects the wording of standard marriage vows. Although the commitment to sexual monogamy is central to most marriages, it remains only a tacit agreement—because of taboos against mentioning sex in a public ceremony. This hushed treatment of sexual commitment sometimes gives the subconscious impression of marriage as an antisexual institution, especially in sexually modern populations. It causes a wide perception that most sex happens outside marriage.

Hosts of the sex-talk taboo can feel as distressed with sexual writing as with sexual conversation. So hosts of the taboo may experience adverse reactions to the sexual topics of this very book, and even the present topic. Still, science seeks to understand phenomena, even where culture discourages it.

When taboos against talking about sex become too intense, they may lose replication indirectly. The most intense meme hosts actually have trouble teaching *their own sex taboos* to offspring until after the children start violating them. By then, it's usually too late. With the sex taboos being violated, the taboo against talking about sex seems alien, and readily ignored. So the sex-talk taboo can diminish transmission of parental-mode memes, itself included. Once this happens on a large scale, natural selection acts to reestablish prevalence for parentally replicating memes. Sex-talk taboos can thus promote society's oscillation between permissive and restrictive attitudes.

CONSUMMATION

The act of mating brings forth one of the simplest quantity parental memes: the idea that sex "consummates" the relationship. This traditional meme, along with memes forbidding low-fertility sex, prods couples to begin parenthood soon after marriage. And whenever one of the meme's hosts marries someone who continues to refuse sex, the host has a memetic basis for dissolving the union as "unconsummated." By letting that host go on to find a new spouse, the meme thus raises its host's average procreation, letting "consummation" propagate.

5

SUCCESSFUL CULTS: WESTERN RELIGION BY NATURAL SELECTION

The true God, the all-powerful God,
is the God of ideas.
—ALFRED VICTOR

An African clan honors its ancestral spirits. Muslims facing Mecca proclaim, "God is great." South American Evangelicals meet for Bible study, while North American Jews read from the Torah. The world bustles with religion—because religions effectively harness human activity toward belief propagation.

ANCESTOR WORSHIP

Ancestor worship promotes reproduction, thus proliferating the belief that deceased ancestors still dominate the living. In many

African and Asian belief systems, powerful ancestors desire to have as many live, worshiping descendants as possible. Fearing for their crops and livestock, the living try to obey their ancestors' will. The belief system thus dictates both high fertility and effective parent-to-child transmission for the belief system.

To please the spirits even more, the living want to make sure that *all* the ancestor's descendants do their part in worship. This motivates people to spread ancestor worship ideas to relatives other than just children and grandchildren. Some may indeed imagine that ancestors favor those who spread the word most—another incentive for proselytizing kin.

Ancestor worship memes also tell hosts that they, too, will enjoy being worshiped in the afterlife. The one catch is that the host must first leave surviving offspring. So the meme neatly promotes both high fertility and belief propagation. These replication advantages continue for ancestor worship in modern peoples, even with the recent superimposing of Christian and Islamic ideas.

MULTIPLE GODS, SINGLE GODS

Almost any belief in a powerful spirit motivates conversion of family and friends. Ancient farmers spread fertility god memes to achieve mutual help in appeasing those gods. Beliefs in sea gods spread widely among coastal peoples for similar reasons. The same motives for proselytizing friends and family recur for countless other gods and spirits. The beliefs also offer a comforting sense of comprehension for many phenomena. Any one person can hold many such beliefs, so polytheism arises inevitably.

Still, retransmitting each god meme requires the believer to spend time in talk and ritual. When one person believes in many gods, the time and effort add up.

Against a thriving polytheistic background, any particular

god meme that grabs a major share of a believer's faculties increases its competitive propagation. With enough time, someone inevitably chances upon a new meme realizing that advantage. "I am the Lord thy God. Thou shalt have no false gods before me" supremely realizes this competition-suppressing advantage. Thus arises the archetype of modern monotheism, right at the top of the Ten Commandments.

JUDAISM

Monotheism constrained hosts of the Yahweh god meme to give all their religious education and conversion efforts to that one god meme. With the help of that advantage, the Yahweh meme eventually displaced polytheistic ideas among the ancient Hebrews.

The one-god meme also helped the evolution of a single, unified code of conduct: a religiously based system of law and morality. Under the one-god system, no one wonders whether different gods demand opposite behaviors. That moral clarity combines with beliefs in divine "law enforcement" and divine omniscience to give compelling drives for obeying the codes of conduct, even when other mortals cannot detect violations. This bolsters the populating action of customs ranging from the dietary to the marital—an indirect advantage in populating the very faith itself.

Populating the Chosen

In two of the simplest examples of self-populating faith, the Genesis commandments to "be fruitful and multiply" and "populate the Earth abundantly and multiply in it" stimulate their own proliferation.

Arguably, ancient Hebrew leaders may have created such "divine commandments" for political, economic, or military reasons. Yet they might just as easily have started when a mother tried to persuade her adult children to make her a grand-mother. The statements certainly appear to have been created all at once for a purpose, but then, so do the structures arising from biological evolution. The true origins may be far richer than any "act of creation" scenario. Humans have spoken per-haps a *billion billion* sentences, enough to accommodate a more *evolutionary* origin like the speculative one offered here:

> 240,000 to 150,000 years ago: Humans evolve a cultural valuation of fertility. People who value fertility simply pass their values down to more children than those who don't, even though the connection between sex and birth is not yet recognized. (For example, men might stick with the women who happen to have high birth rates.)
>
> 150,000 years ago: Someone coins the goodwill salutation, "Be fruitful and fertile," much as an alien might coin the salutation "Live long and prosper."
>
> 10,000 years ago: With nascent agriculture come methods of reckoning for ownership and exchange. New terms like *add* and *multiply* enter the lexicon and begin to spread.
>
> 9,000 years ago: A host of the now-widespread saying "Be fruitful and fertile" utters the sentence "Be fruitful and multiply" as a variant salutation. A few people start imitat-ing it for its novelty.
>
> 8,990 years ago: A patriarch or matriarch says, "Be fruitful and multiply" as a commandment to all the children and grandchildren. Some of them copy the practice, and the clan starts to grow. Other clans to whom the "Be fruitful and multiply" *salutation* has diffused follow similar paths.
>
> 7,000 years ago: Vast tribes and clans live by the adage "Be fruitful and multiply."

5,000 years ago: Early monotheism emerges. Adherents begin to attribute verses and proverbs to the deity.

4,900 years ago: With thousands of verses and proverbs already attributed to the deity, someone attributes "Be fruitful and multiply" to the deity as well. That attribution gives the commandment more force, resulting in more reproduction.

4,000 years ago: Variants of monotheism attributing "Be fruitful and multiply" to the deity now predominate, having outpopulated the other variants.

Regardless of how the "go multiply" memes started, they were thought contagions waiting to happen: beliefs that would inevitably outlive their first proponents and outpropagate whatever original purposes they might have had.

"Populate the earth" instructions must have flourished in synergy with the old idea of Hebrews as the chosen people. The latter, after all, gives hosts an explanation for their divine duty to be fruitful and multiply. Even if scripture had not specified the belief explicitly, people might well have inferred the "go multiply" ideas from the "chosen people" meme. So the "chosen people" meme fosters parental dissemination, both through its own power and in symbiosis with the "go multiply" memes.

Of course, inclusion among God's chosen also feels good. This gives the meme emotional appeal. Newly exposed non-hosts may desire to adopt the "chosen people" meme for its morale benefit, and many existing hosts cling to the meme for the comfort and pride it confers.

Yet the "chosen people" meme can diminish proselytism, by implying that not everyone should convert to the faith. Moreover, exposed nonhosts may resent their implied designation as "unchosen," hardening them against conversion and even provoking hostility against believers. The meme thus trades off its fertility enhancements against proselytism and even survival losses.

Moral Commandments

Inclusion in the "chosen people" certainly comes with moral strings attached, including a "top ten" list attributed directly to God. The first three of the Ten Commandments act fairly directly to spread the faith, commandments and all. The command to recognize only the Hebrew god helps the faith spread by concentrating faith-spreading efforts on Judaism alone. The injunction against taking the Lord's name in vain causes adherents to express more respectful messages about their faith. And the call for a weekly Lord's day sets aside time to spread and preserve the faith.

The admonition to honor father and mother elevates parenthood to a position of honor, promoting a key route to faith replication. Hosts of this meme would presumably raise more children and therefore pass their religious commandments down to more descendants. The meme also presents parents with an obvious motive for spreading the meme: to get more respect and obedience from their children. In this regard, the meme derives more fitness as a message from God than it could as a message from mere parents. If "Honor your parents" were presented as the parents' idea, then children could reject it as a mere ploy. Expecting this in advance, parents would see the purely secular meme as less useful to pass down than its "Lord-spoken" counterpart. "Honor your parents" thus thrives on parental replication—especially as a religious tenet.

Sacred Marriage

In another parentally vigorous feature, Judaism and many other faiths incorporate marriage itself into religious custom. This helps replicate the faith by discouraging divorce. Divorced people usually lose time from their reproductive careers, so dissuading couples from divorce promotes the birth of more children and more parental transmission for the religion.

A divorce can also separate the children from one of the parents, reducing meme transmission rates from the missing parent. If the children stay with the mother, the sons may miss the transmission of parentally prolific male-role memes from the father, and similarly for daughters staying with the father. By preventing such transmission losses, the religious preservation of marriage again augments propagation of the whole faith.

The specific commandment against adultery likewise flourishes through parental transmission. By preventing broken families and absentee parenthood, the taboo improves its own retransmission into believers' progeny. It does this especially well as a commandment from God, the omniscient enforcer. Without the omniscient enforcement idea, many more would violate the taboo when they thought they could escape detection by mortals. So the god meme helps the taboo gain young adherents, and the taboo helps the god meme gain young adherents. Other sex and mating mores achieve similar replication synergy with the god meme, explaining how such morals become intensely bound up in religion.

The adultery taboo also spreads by proselytism *between adults*. Hosts voice the meme both to spouses they want to keep faithful and to third parties they want to exclude sexually. And because the omniscient enforcer idea affords better deterrence, they often express their taboo as a commandment from God instead of as a secular idea. Religion and morality again spread synergistically.

Other Morals

Moral codes against killing, stealing, and slandering enjoy very similar replication advantages. Anyone who wishes to avoid violent death feels motivated to tell others not to kill. Anyone who wants to keep his or her belongings feels inclined to morally educate offspring and others against theft, and so forth. Such motives work to spread morality memes in settings ranging from ancient paganism to modern secularism. Still, expressing them as *God's* morals becomes attractive as a way of seeking better compliance—and hence more safety from murder, theft, and slander. The morals, therefore, add further incentives for spreading the faith. Added replication drive, in turn, makes natural selection favor moralistic religions such as Judaism.

When morality becomes incorporated in religion, it generates still another motive for expressing the faith: to gain others' trust and the attendant socioeconomic benefits. Highly moral people, for instance, can express faith in a moralistic religion to gain *recognition* as moral. Yet many immoral people also express faith in moralistic religions, both to acquire camouflage and to exploit the unsuspecting. But *both* phenomena can spread the faith, and both probably helped moralistic varieties gain ascendancy in early Judaism.

Once a moralistic faith establishes itself as a way to impart morals to children, it also becomes hard for young adults to drop out permanently. Those brought up with religious morality can have little or no experience with other methods of raising an ethical, socially adjusted child. So even if they *try* to drop the faith in early adulthood, they experience strong forces pulling them back as they start their own families. This would have helped Judaism retain its adherents in ancient times, and it helps Judeo-Christian faiths retain adherents in modern times: an almost timeless propagation advantage.

Dietary Laws

Jewish dietary laws may have helped populate the faith under primitive conditions. Laws against eating shellfish, pork, and other parasite-laden animals may reduce mortality rates, thus propagating the movement. Without knowledge of parasitology, divine punishment ideas can still stop both secret and overt pork consumption. This can protect people regardless of whether they recognize a connection between disease and certain foods. If they see the connection, then "divine punishment" helps them explain it; if they overlook the connection, "divine punishment" affords "blind" protection still favored by natural selection. Fear of God's wrath also fuels proselytism of divine dietary laws to friends and relatives, augmenting the ideas' proliferation.

Finally, the food taboos inhibit conversion to competing faiths by making it harder for Jews to fit in to Gentile cultures—a faith-propagating advantage even for dietary laws lacking any hygienic advantage.

Faith, Devotion, Collective Punishment, and Scripture

Belief in collective punishment for unfaithfulness immunizes hosts from disillusionment during hard times. Whenever such hardships as famine strike, many adherents develop doubts about the faith. Those with mass divine punishment in their belief sets have a ready explanation for the trouble and so remain steady believers; those lacking this meme often drop the whole faith. Each calamity's dropouts enrich the concentration of remaining Jews who accept the collective punishment creed. Indeed, these people have memetic reasons for redoubling their faith whenever hardship strikes. They might even work to redouble the faith of others in order to relieve the collective punishment, adding copreservation and proselytic strengths to the "collective punishment" meme. So the Jews' repeated hardships have fostered the belief in divine mass punishment, which in turn fosters the continued success of the Judaic belief set.

Another ancient memetic innovation safeguarding Jewish belief is the fundamental concept of faith itself. Whenever the religion seems to defy reason, the senses, or emotions, those believers who memetically value faith often remain in the religion while others drop out. Their religion also survives more pressures to join alternative ideologies, including other religions. So whether or not it can move mountains, faith certainly prevents believers from seriously questioning or leaving the religion. This enriches the incidence of the faith idea in those who remain with the religion and gives the religion a competitive edge against others that lack the doctrine of faith.

The innovation of holy scripture also preserved Hebrew religious memes against dropout by restoring lapses of memory, while improving transmission fidelity to upcoming generations. This meme transmission tool gave hosts more chance of success in passing the memes on to others by expanding the number of people they could reach. Writing also achieved a higher degree of transmission accuracy, or *copying fidelity,* as Richard Dawkins called it in *The Selfish Gene.* Greater accuracy boosts the percentage of new hosts correctly indoctrinated while suppressing accidental competing variations from arising in the process. The combined advantages have made scripture one of the most successful innovations in all of religious history, while expanding the *realm* of literacy as well.

Finally, the idea of "devoting one's life to the Lord" greatly boosts propagation by amplifying all the other propagation mechanisms of the faith. Regardless of whether there actually is a "Lord" to appreciate the devoted humans, hosts of the devotion idea pay very high service to the body of ideas they attribute to "the Lord." This usually results in high performance at preserving, elucidating, and transmitting the entire religion's belief set, including incidentally the devotion to the Lord meme. So the meme advances itself as a central feature of Judaism and its descendant faiths.

CHRISTIANITY

Christianity is the largest offshoot from the phylogenetic root of Judaism. It grew to overshadow its parent faith by retaining most of the Jewish propagation features and adding some new and potent ones of its own.

The idea that every host should go forth and "preach the gospel to all" added enormously to the religion's proselytic advantages in both its early days and many later periods. Indeed, during the severe Roman persecution of dissenters, the only movements that could flourish were those that somehow spread fast enough to offset repression's depopulating effects. Christianity, with all its proselytic vigor, thus expanded despite heavy losses among its founder, early leaders, and disciples.

Several supporting memes boost Christianity's phenomenal proselytic drive. For instance, Christianity contains strong ideas that God rewards belief with eternal salvation and punishes unbelief with eternal damnation. This means that hosts need to convert all who matter to them before they die. Taken alone, the meme provides considerable motivation to proselytize. It also creates a faith-preservation advantage by threatening hosts with infinite losses if they drop out. So heaven and hell adherents proselytize more and drop out less.

Heaven and hell ideas also give proselytizing Christians leverage over the nonhost's receptivity to persuasion. Hearing the dire eternal consequences of continued unbelief and the wonderful rewards of belief can lure the newly exposed into treating questions of truth as questions of risk. As the beliefs imply infinite loss for erroneous rejection but no loss for erroneous acceptance, the newly exposed often decide in favor of conversion. In short, the beliefs manipulate their own risk management impact, thereby gaining persuadability from the newly exposed.

Augmenting the risk treatment of belief are the sincere but contagious worries of those who proselytize. Whenever they show their fear for an unbeliever's afterlife fate, they help stir up similar fears in the unbeliever. The unbeliever might otherwise give little attention and worry to the subject, meaning that the host does not merely play upon existing death worries, but helps create them and amplify them. Indeed, the spreading of death worries along with the religious doctrine makes it difficult to say just how much people dwell on death without cultural suggestion. The phenomenon shows how memes can boost the receptivity they encounter by making adherents change an unbeliever's mood.

"Christian love" expands on the proselytic power of heaven and hell ideas. The "Love your neighbor as yourself" idea means that anyone, indeed, everyone warrants your efforts to "save" them. So the meme broadens its hosts' proselytic horizons well beyond established family and friends.

Besides urging Christians to preach to more listeners, "Christian love" can win more receptivity per listener. The loving treatment of nonhosts by proselytizers can persuade them that the proselytism itself demonstrates loving concern. Convinced that proselytism is meant for their own good, nonhosts move a big step closer to trusting it enough to accept it. Once again, a meme actively sways the emotional receptivity of newly exposed nonhosts.

Though it refers to a general "neighbor" in the third person, the "Love your neighbor" meme also helps people tell others, by implication, "Love me as you love yourself." This, of course, gives the host a purely selfish reason for retransmitting the meme, even if most only feel the motive subconsciously.

Though the love message can become a vehicle for exploiting true believers, it can also set up a community of mutually cooperating believers. By giving its host population the socioeconomic benefits of cooperation, the meme probably causes a net improvement in their quality of life. Robert Axelrod's *The Evolution of Cooperation* posits that cooperation can evolve purely from the recursive imitation of those who prosper from it. The "Love your neighbor" meme accelerates that evolution by spreading cooperation as a proselytic meme package.

On the congregation level, "Love your neighbor" can help prevent dropouts. By suppressing serious conflict, the meme stops churches from splitting up and members from going away mad. Since departing members can more easily lose faith, the Christian love meme gives a preservation advantage to the whole faith.

Extremely altruistic behavior sometimes follows from combining the idea of life devoted to the Lord with the belief that the Lord commands universal love. Faithful hosts of this combination can make exceptional to spectacular achievements in charity. The wide recognition and favorable attention given to those special believers provide them an attentive audience for the transmission and imitation of faith. Since most people crave attention and recognition, such special believers also tacitly display a potential reward for conversion. Long-time believers may feel drawn to imitating the highest levels of devotion, too. Some "audience" members even see the correlation between faith and charity as evidence for the divine presence espoused by the faithful. This adds some cognitive potency to the beliefs of the faithful. Thus, the universal love meme increases both the transmissivity and the receptivity of Christianity. "Love your neighbor" does double duty in memetic natural selection—and provides favors for humanity as well.

Apocalypse and Rapture

Apocalypse and rapture beliefs in the Biblical book of Revelation reinforce the proselytic subsystem centered on heaven and hell ideas. The apocalypse idea makes hosts "realize" that very little time remains to "save" all the neighbors they love, as mentioned in chapter one. Early Christianity thus propagated vigorously under the added urgency of an apocalypse meme. Yet the continued nonoccurrence of an apocalypse tends to provoke cognitive immune reactions against the meme, leading many to drop the meme or modify it to the point of practical irrelevance. Occasionally, a new variant of Christianity reinstates the old apocalypse meme, causing those new movements to spread until their own apocalyptic forecasts start to fail.

The belief in a divine "rapture" works similarly. In this meme, hosts believe that God will soon come and spirit away all true Christians to heaven just before apocalyptic happenings. Like the imminent apocalypse meme, this belief shortens its hosts' perceived deadline for evangelical efforts, thus urgently accelerating the proselytism. Yet the meme also alleviates apocalyptic worry for believers by assuring their escape from the hardship. This makes daily life easier. And with less stress from constantly expecting the end, they may find it easier to retain those end-time ideas for decades. The rapture belief thus promotes long-term survival for itself and the apocalypse meme during a mundanely persistent earth time.

Crucifixion

The belief that Jesus suffered and died to save humanity gained a defining role in Christianity by amplifying all the faith's replication advantages at once. The meme tells its hosts that they owe virtually everything—especially their eternal salvation—to Christ the Savior. This makes them willing to do whatever it takes to please their Savior in return. In practice, it means doing almost anything to serve those *beliefs* attributed to the Savior. So Christians willingly make the enormous sacrifices of missionary work, crusades, holy wars, evangelism, big families, ministry, and so forth. The message that Jesus died for our sins gets itself profusely retransmitted in the process, accounting for its vast prevalence today.

So robust is the Redemption on the Cross meme that other memes gain replication power just by reinforcing it. In particular, a belief in the Eucharist causes Christians to periodically relive the account of Jesus sacrificing body and blood for the salvation of human beings. These recurrent reenactments remind believers of their indebtedness to the Savior—and thus to any messages they attribute to him. Having *personally* accepted this sacrifice in Communion also makes the believer feel *individually* indebted to the Savior. This can elicit even more "return sacrifice" for the faith, helping it spread faster. Holy Communion thus ascends to its prominent place in the lives of most Christians.

The placement of crucifixes at home, church, or elsewhere likewise reminds Christians of their redemption on the cross meme. Crosses that graphically depict a dying Jesus work especially well at reminding believers of the immense sacrifice the Savior made for them, and implicitly repeat the call for a return sacrifice to the faith. Crosses and cross-display memes thus become the most common signs of Christianity around the world.

The crucifixion meme does, however, leave Christianity and its believers more vulnerable to exploitation from unbelievers and greedy professionals. Phony religious leaders use the crucifixion meme to generate guilt-inspired contributions, as can half-sincere leaders who spend lavishly on themselves. This weakens the movement as some members catch on and drop out. Yet even desires to exploit Christianity give a parasitic leader motives to spread the core beliefs, including the crucifixion meme. So parasites become symbionts to a degree, and the movement continues.

Resurrection

As a young movement, Christianity achieved a phenomenal proselytic meme complex: a belief in preaching to all, supported by the intensifying ideas of heaven, hell, love, apocalypse, and rapture. Against this background, the central belief in resurrection becomes less of a mystery.

Assume for the moment that a historical Jesus actually did start the movement and was indeed executed by the Romans. Many followers become disillusioned and drop out. Yet among the most loyal followers, a few are eventually heard to proclaim, "Jesus lives!" much as extreme Elvis fans currently proclaim, "Elvis lives!"

The "Jesus lives" crowd continue spreading the faith, spurred on by an intact proselytic system of memes attributed to Jesus. Eventually, they come to outnumber the disillusioned followers who believe that Jesus died an ordinary, irreversible death.

With continued growth, the "Jesus lives" population expands enough to exhibit variations in the details of belief. Some, for instance, believe that "Jesus never died," while others believe that, "Jesus died, but rose again."

These variations have real differences in how much importance to assign to Jesus' teachings: the idea that he died and rose again implies far more importance than the idea that he never really died. So among the "Jesus lives" population, the resurrectionist subset begins to grow and eventually takes over the movement.

Within the resurrectionist movement, still more variations

arise, with any that support resurrectionism outreplicating those that don't. Thus, we end up with a faith that includes not only the idea of resurrection, but numerous supporting ideas: witness accounts, scriptural fulfillment beliefs, and so forth. The process continues even in modern times, as people who see resurrection proved by the Shroud of Turin outproselytize those who accept its carbon[14] dating as a thirteenth-century artifact. Natural selection lives!

Evil Apostasy

Proselytizing exposes Christians to many varied beliefs, and even to contrary proselytism. Therefore, Christians with memes that immunize them against contrary views stay Christian the longest. A belief that un-Christian messages are evil, even Satanical, is one such preservational meme. Christian hosts of this doctrine generally react with extreme distrust toward anyone expressing a contrary belief. That leads them to discard the contrary messages and remain Christian. This memetic immune mechanism thus confers preservational advantage to each faith that incorporates it, including Christianity.

An "evil apostasy" meme sometimes goes well beyond conferring memetic immunity, inspiring cases of religious aggression. In severe historical cases, Christian aggression helps depopulate contrary belief systems, boosting the faith's net "market share." Even if aggression against unbelievers only represses their free *expression,* it still limits the competitors' propagation.

Christianity originally lacked such an adversative advantage, as its first three centuries occurred during the pagan days of Roman military rule. That channeled Christianity's evolutionary course toward proselytically spread memes like universal love. Of course, gaining control of the Roman empire and later governments freed Christianity to evolve more aggressive strains. Yet the early evolutionary legacy of loving proselytism seems to mollify that potential in various regions and eras.

The big evolutionary drawback of the "evil apostasy" doctrine arises when competing religions or competing varieties of Christianity apply it to each other. Here, the most mutually intolerant believers tend to kill each other off or destroy each other's livelihoods. The intolerant volunteer in higher proportions for dangerous warfare roles, where they frequently meet their deadly counterparts in the opposing faith. Survival on each side thus ensues most often to people with tolerant doctrines. Moreover, those tolerant believers in each sect who fear becoming new conscripts feel motivated to preach tolerance in order to spare their own lives. This gives proselytic strength to protolerance memes during times of actual religious strife. All these factors help explain the modern rise of religious pluralism in much of the world. Ideas of "evil apostasy" still propagate, but mostly within the limits of pluralism.

Interfaith Marriage Taboos

While contempt for apostasy may discourage religious intermarriage, specific taboos also work against such unions. These intermarriage taboos spread under their own power.

An intermarriage taboo pressures its religious hosts (Christian or other) to convert any serious prospective mate. In this context, Christianity acts as a romantically and sexually transmitted belief. The taboo's proselytic effect enjoys leveraged receptivity, since the courtship partner must convert or lose a relationship. The proselytic audience, though small, becomes a rich source of converts.

Proselytic advantages advance the similar taboos in Judaism and Islam. Once intermarriage bans become mutual, members of each faith have trouble finding *serious* marital prospects from each other's ranks. Ironically, this drives down the very proselytic advantages that fostered the taboos in the first place. It even leads to mutually canceling marital conversion rates, where the faiths win a trickle of spouses from each other.

In this setting, the intermarriage taboo takes on a new preservational advantage. The taboo stops believers from converting to other faiths by leading to a standoff instead. So even though marital conversions diminish, Christianity and other faiths still achieve better host retention by continuing to forbid intermarriage.

The taboo also helps Christianity spread from parents to children by promoting *homogamy*—religious agreement between spouses. Couples of greatly different faiths may leave children feeling unconvinced that *either* parent is correct, reducing the religious imitation ratio. Imitating *neither* parent occurs more often when parents strongly disagree. Homogamy prevents this result, favoring more reliable parent–to–child religion transfer.

The religious homogamy preference also spreads itself by fostering greater partner consensus on how to conduct relationships, since religions codify many family and mating norms. Metaphorically, homogamous couples carry compatible packages of "prebundled marital software." They tend to agree more on child raising, birth control, sex taboos, and so forth. The more restrictive the religion, the more exactly its homogamous couples concur on such matters. They even concur more on how to resolve any disputes that still arise. The religious doctrines placing the husband at head of household with higher rule going to the clergy or the Bible can settle most disputes, even if one sex gets the better deal. These memes, then, can reduce overt strife and divorce among hosts. In turn, marital stability favors more reproduction and the successful indoctrination of children.

Yet rigid homogamy memes sometimes interfere with mate selection, increasing the average nuptial age. Hosts simply have fewer potential mates, especially in religiously mixed communities. The extra time spent searching for an eligible mate tends to reduce the average number of children. This parental transmission loss prevents an unlimited proliferation and strictness of intermarriage taboos. In the United States, it usually means fairly free intermarriage between similar Christian denominations. Mating becomes more restricted with differences such as Catholic to Protestant or mainline to evangelical marriages. Intermarriage becomes quite taboo with differences as great as Catholic to Jewish or Jewish to Muslim pairings.

Roman Catholic Europe

Christianity's great proselytic expansion throughout medieval Europe eventually saturated that continent. So many people heard "the Word" that immunity to conversion replaced nonexposure as the prevailing reason for unbelief, among Jews, for instance. Put another way, the survival of unbelief depended so much on resistance to Christianity that memetic immunity evolved by natural selection among the other religions.

Christians had fewer and fewer local—hence real—opportunities for winning converts. For all practical purposes, they had no one to proselytize but each other, and there was no propagation advantage in that. The proselytic zeal of Christianity faced evolutionary atrophy. Ideas that had previously led their hosts to proselytize became mere inspirations to waste time or even lives, as in the Crusades. So the memes of proselytic zeal began dwindling toward extinction.

With most proselytic opportunity spent, only parental propagation mattered greatly. Ideas that promoted having and raising more children still vigorously outpropagated those that did not. With parental transmission advantages dominating, an especially rich body of parental-mode memes evolved in the Roman Catholic Church during that time. The few remaining roles for nonparental dissemination evolved into the propagation specialist jobs of the clergy.

The situation had shifted drastically from the early days of Christianity, when each additional proselytic effort worked so well that net propagation actually increased when believers gave up reproduction to live the life of itinerant preaching. As proselytic saturation set in, the idea of giving up reproduction evolved into its more restricted form, which applied only to preaching specialists such as priests and nuns.

Reformation and Revival

The Church's evolution away from proselytic vigor and toward parental-mode vigor gave opportunities for upstart religious variants to spread by renewing those dormant proselytic ideas. An accumulation of clerical parasites further weakened it by giving members reason to leave. While various "heresies" *did* spring up and propagate during the Middle Ages, the first with enough proselytic vigor to endure extensive persecution was the Protestant Reformation.

As the Reformation spread, it eventually created enclaves where Protestants, too, faced a local shortage of potential converts, leading to proselytic stagnation and atrophy. That in turn set the stage for reformations within reformations. This provides one of the memetic causes for speciation and subspeciation of Protestantism into its diverse denominations.

The idea of breaking off from the established movement also accelerated speciation. Once Martin Luther broke from the Roman Catholic Church, his followers implicitly formed a stronger idea of leading breakaway movements of their own. Although Christianity was itself an offshoot of Judaism, Catholic doctrine held that there could only be one such "legitimate" break. Luther implicitly legitimized the idea of multiple breaks, and further break-offs began in two decades with the birth of Calvinism.

Since the oldest Protestant movements have had more time to reach proselytic atrophy, evangelical varieties are usually newer denominations. Yet repeated waves of evangelical revival can also sweep through an established denomination, with each revival movement reaching its own proselytic atrophy and fading back to the calm that favors a subsequent revival outbreak.

Scriptural Proselytism

Gutenberg's invention of movable-type printing helped determine what sort of movement could emerge to challenge the Roman Catholic Church, for it allowed wide access to vernacular Bibles. Though early Christians had to orally impart their entire faith to most new converts, the early Protestants could spread their beliefs by telling people to consult a centrally printed text. That text, in turn, told them to retransmit their faith. Hence the great replication advantage to Biblically oriented movements such as those led by Luther, Calvin, and many since.

An analogy exists for a computer virus that can use the centrally disseminated software of an operating system to effect its own replication. Such a computer virus need not carry all the instructions needed for copying files, but can instead tell its host computer to "go to" a program already accessible. Likewise, the post-Gutenberg evangelist could almost tell a listener to "go to the Bible" rather than lecturing on the specifics of faith.

Of course, the Bible doesn't work *quite* so easily as computer software. Along with a "go to the Bible" instruction come various instructions for *interpreting* the text, including what parts to read first, what parts to emphasize, and what parts to deemphasize. Evangelists can impart much of this directly, and still more by telling the convert to "go to such and such church" or "refer to such and such catechism."

Natural selection can thus operate on competing varieties of *interpretation* without giving rise to wildly different Bibles. And while the business of printing and distributing Bibles looks like centralized communication, the transmission of religious belief retains its character as a grass-roots phenomenon.

Instant Rewards

The most proselytic denominations, the evangelicals, tend toward belief in instant rewards for conversion. The ideas of spiritual "joy" and "abundant living" here on earth tend to boost the listener's receptivity to evangelical persuasion. The idea that Christians gain influence over God's actions through prayer likewise appeals to any who feel impatient about waiting until death for conversion rewards.

On hearing the claims of instant rewards, nonbelievers feel tempted to at least try the faith. Indeed, the promises often combine with a meme stating that one can *only* test the faith by adopting it. Hostship then activates numerous preservational mechanisms—regardless of actual "test" results. So the proclaimed incentives for "trying" the faith often produce lasting conversions.

In order for the life improvement promises to impress nonhosts, proselytizers must outwardly appear delighted with their lives. The memes about "joy" and "abundant living" can accomplish this through self-fulfilling prophecy. Most people become happy just from the *expectation* of happiness and reward. The memes can also cause people to simply *choose* a happier outlook. It all adds up to a transmissible package of belief attractants.

Easy versus Hard Salvation

Easy salvation augments proselytism as another belief-attracting promise. "Easy salvation" means that being saved depends only on converting to the faith. This includes such memetic variations as "accepting Christ as Lord" or "adopting a personal relationship with Jesus Christ." These faith-based salvation memes motivate hosts to just get the nonhosts converted, because then the eternal benefits seem assured. It also offers more appeal to the prospective convert, with eternal rewards assured regardless of good works or pious living.

Yet "difficult" salvation can prevent dropouts. Believers in salvation through good works and piety often try to live accordingly. So they may have emotional barriers against switching to a faith that diminishes the importance of all their past efforts. All the different strengths of "easy" and "difficult" salvation play themselves out to yield the wide range of actual beliefs within Christendom.

Symbolic Expressions

Emotional symbols provide other potent adhesives for retaining believers. The music, art, ceremony, celebration, and fellowship of religious communities can so move the congregation as to "confirm" the faith to its members. Congregations achieving the most emotionally fulfilling culture can thus grow by longer membership retention. The phenomenon fosters some high aesthetic achievements in the Christian world.

The practice of putting the creed to song also proliferates through its mnemonic advantages. People remember words they sing better than words plainly spoken, so religious song helps adherents remember what they believe and reduces their dropout rates.

Christianity also spreads with the help of small symbols.

Prayers before meals tend to announce Christianity to all those present. Since meals serve important social gathering functions, prayers at mealtime tend to reveal one's faith to most of one's close acquaintances. The believer sees the purpose as thankfulness to God, but the custom's evolutionary adaptation is its advertising value. The mealtime prayer meme can even self-advertise to Christians who still lack just that specific meme. It thus spreads both as a single thought contagion and as part of the larger Christian meme package.

The practice of wearing crosses likewise helps spread the faith to non-Christians, and the cross-wearing meme itself to other Christians. The symbol in this case stays on the faithful during virtually all their encounters with others, letting it reap example-display transmissions.

Growth Wins Attention

Once natural selection produces a very quickly growing church, denomination, or movement, the rapid growth becomes an attention getter in its own right. Outsiders sit up and take notice, and today's media come in to cover the story as a news event. This in turn helps the movement evangelize to a larger audience, adding further to its growth.

Among the most attentive, at least in modern times, are the ministers and leaders of slow-growing and dwindling movements. With their jobs and careers at stake, they often go looking for a success formula in a thriving congregation and try to replicate it in their own flocks. This can further spread ideas of biblical literalism, easy salvation, and so forth.

Yet ministers hold limited power over their followers. A single person cannot easily inspire fervent evangelism in a crowd that traditionally avoids it. Thus, recent efforts by the clergy to restore evangelism to the Catholic population fell on mostly deaf ears. Sensing expansion motives among the clergy, parishioners often leave the drudgery of proselytism up to them. So the faith remains adapted to mainly parental transmission, with little that priests can do about it. Natural selection continues its "design" work on an essentially bottom-up, rather than top-down basis.

Denomination and Class

The historically wide range of Christian attitudes toward the material world helps endow the memberships of different sects with different material fortunes. Additionally, high-fertility sects may subdivide inheritance and other advantages more than do low-fertility sects, again leading to average social class differences. Such differences form the more *direct* economic consequences of religious belief.

Yet sects also stratify by social class through the interactions of religious "software" with social class "software." These interactions generally dampen proselytism among the middle to upper classes. The maxim that "You are judged by the company you keep" operates widely among people striving to project middle-class images, while social climbing often involves cultivating powerful friends. This plus discomforts between "haves" and "have-nots" can leave the status-minded feeling inhibited from "social promiscuity." When an evangelical asks them to convert, the status-minded realize that the duty to proselytize would give them more contact with lower classes and compromise their social exclusivity. Hence, they often have an immune reaction to the evangelical message. Associating the low-status role of solicitor with evangelism may also trigger class-conscious immunity to evangelical Christianity. These dynamics help limit the evangelical penetration into upper middle classes. Genuine desires for *privacy* can make the proselytizing life even more unthinkable in the upper strata.

Besides reactions against the obligation to proselytize,

evangelical and other memetically vigorous sects can lose social class appeal by proliferating to the point of commonality. Personal images of exclusivity sometimes suffer from involvement in highly inclusive denominations.

Through their reliance on the Bible, which exalts the poor, evangelicals may win extra converts from lower classes. This invites still more class stereotyping and intensifies the social distance desired by the higher classes.

Despite the different class affiliations and proselytic goals among Christian denominations, many started as evangelical movements, and all have descended from the highly evangelical beginnings of Christianity. As mentioned earlier, the cooling of proselytic zeal among formerly evangelical faiths results partly from proselytic saturation. Yet socioeconomic advancement of adherents and their descendants may also play a part. As their status increases, individuals and families experience social and economic pressure to limit their associations and hence their proselytism. So old denominations launched evangelically now contain many families who feel more socially restrained from proselytizing than did their less established ancestors. This adds still another class factor impeding the total predominance of evangelical denominations.

Social class differences affect not only the rate and zeal, but also the manner of proselytism. Though not considered "evangelical," mainline Protestant churchgoers often "proselytize" by inviting their friends along. For class-oriented churches, the art, music, and architecture can make a favorable impression before any preaching starts. Without any "hard sell," the church full of worshiping believers provides ample conformity pressure to make a new visitor join in praying aloud. As visitors recite prayers and sing hymns, a desire to believe one's own voice helps them convert to full believers. What begins as a polite invitation to church ends in propagating the creed. Offering a mere invitation also violates fewer social status principles, making it a viable means of religious thought contagion among classes that reject overt evangelism.

The social strata thus make diverse evolutionary niches fostering various modes of faith transmission—modes derived through generations of denominations adapting by natural selection.

Religion and the Sexes

Most Christian propagation advantages work fairly symmetrically between the sexes. Yet Christianity has achieved greater prevalence and intensity among women than among men in North America, suggesting that at least some of its contagion value works differently for each sex.

Traditional social science might look for sex differences in emotional receptivity or critical thinking to explain the differences in religiosity. Memetics can suggest entirely new principles behind the religious gender gap.

Gender-skewed proselytism during mating offers one memetic explanation. Religious homogamy memes can lead both sexes to proselytize opposite sex unbelievers in order to make them "eligible." Yet men might do so more assertively than women, at least traditionally, resulting in more conversions of women than men.

Moreover, homogamy memes deter believers from dating the religion's competition, thus defending the faith from out-marriages and deconversions. Catholics with strong homogamy memes seldom take much chance of conversion by Southern Baptist dating partners. But if men do most of the proselytizing, women do most of the listening, making the "defensive" aspect of homogamy run stronger among women. This in turn favors the evolution of more prevalent and intense homogamy memes among women than among men, a difference confirmed in surveys of mating priorities. Stronger homogamy memes in women can, however, make women more assertive proselytists, offsetting some of the male assertiveness that favors strong memes in women.

Intense religiosity can also confer resistance to the sexually motivated proselytism of memes favoring pleasure over reproduction. If men promote such ideas as precommittal sex to women more assertively than vice versa, and if the ideas do diminish reproduction, then religion advances women's reproductive careers more than men's. This would raise the number of daughters emulating a religious woman more than the number of sons emulating a religious man. Accumulating over generations, the effect can preferentially heighten female religiosity.

A deeper reason for gender-correlated religiosity stems from its specific involvement in marriage. Treating marriage as a Christian sacrament automatically defines God as enforcer of the vows. To true believers, this enforcement is inescapable. No serious believer can expect to abandon a spouse or otherwise break the vows and get away with it.

Yet marital security plays a pivotal role in the willingness to have children, especially for women. Women usually stand to suffer much greater material and reproductive loss from desertion than do men. Therefore, any memes that cause female hosts to marry an unshakably vow-abiding husband tend to promote the women's reproductive success. If the memes also help women *perceive* their husbands as unshakably vow-abiding, the resultant *feelings* of reproductive security can promote still more fertility.

When highly religious women achieve homogamy, they can get both the reality of a religiously vow-abiding husband and the secure perceptions as well. Such women may therefore raise more children and act as role models to more daughters than do other women. This gives intense religion greater propagation among females than among males.

These marital effects can easily operate unnoticed by the

faithful. Many see only coherent child raising as a rationale for homogamy; yet they incidentally tend toward marriages that make women feel secure about reproduction. But when people *do* recognize the "vow enforcement" implications of religion, it favors female religiosity even more by increasing the emotional appeal to women more than to men. Homogamous religion wins with women, whether consciously or not.

The success of religion among women gives religious men an advantage at seeking mates. That in turn gives them more reproduction than other men get, ensuring that men never fall vastly behind women in religiosity.

Christianity's vow enforcement provisions may lose some of their expansion advantages with advanced police and court systems to enforce legal marriage. Financially solvent men can no longer easily abandon wives and children without encountering the agencies that collect child support and alimony. So more women might feel secure about reproduction without the traditional threat of divine marriage enforcement hanging over their men. The phenomenon may help let advanced societies drift slightly away from intense religion.

Though Christianity usually describes God as male, a fairly wide range of memetic phenomena make the faith itself more commonly female. Far from settling the issue, memetic theory merely presents a new class of explanations worth investigating.

ISLAM

Islam forms the third great monotheism branching from the Judeo-Christian-Islamic family tree. Over six centuries younger than Christianity, Islam has spread so fast as to closely rival Christianity's following.

Belief in imitating the ways of Mohammed generates some of Islam's proselytic drive, since Mohammed himself won many converts. The mechanism resembles the Christian idea of emulating Jesus, who likewise had a reputation for making converts.

The teaching that God will end the world when its people fall away from Mohammed's teachings also fosters Islamic proselytism. Hosts of this belief see the propagation of faith as potentially a matter of survival, turning survival motives into proselytic drives. More directly, it motivates believers to dissuade each other from losing faith, thereby maintaining Muslim numbers. In the most extreme cases, the belief justifies death penalties for dropping out, heightening the believers' ability to deter dropouts among themselves. It even impedes competing faiths from accumulating former Muslims, another advantage in the religious population race.

The Koranic requirement for public prayer five times a day spreads Islam by enunciating the faith within earshot of nearby non-Muslims. Highly conspicuous body postures and movements bolster the effect by attracting attention. The frequent recitation of these prayers also helps preserve the faith by preventing Muslims from forgetting what they believe. This matters most in historical and modern regions of low literacy, since scriptural "memory" depends on reading.

Jihad

Islam's early growth went unchecked by any great empire constraining its modes of transmission. Unlike Christianity, Islam could therefore incorporate religious warfare memes into its original doctrines. Power, protection, and the spoils of war certainly provided personal expedience for Mohammed's religious and military ideas. Yet the ideas' self-propagation potency gave them their long-term expansion.

Islamic military expansion illustrates the collective effort the faith commands. The faith provides for a *jihad* or holy war, which historically led to Islamic rule over whole societies.

Once a war establishes Islamic law over a new society, that law acts to persuade individuals to become Muslims. Most pagans have no choice but to convert or die. Traditional Islamic law also requires others, notably Christians and Jews, to pay special taxes that end only if they convert or emigrate. This of course motivates conversion by those coming under Islamic rule. It also materially reduces the non-Muslim capacity to raise children and otherwise transmit competing faiths, while boosting the material advantages to Islam. With time, the Islamic laws thereby render territories overwhelmingly Muslim.

The memetic promise of paradise for anyone who dies fighting for Islam gives the faith some of its historical expansion strength, too. The idea not only inspires bravery during military battle, but also promotes lifelong civilian struggle for Islam to ensure that the moment of death occurs during the struggle—thus assuring paradise. As with Christianity and Judaism, paradise assured for the devout means expansion secured for the belief set.

When men die fighting for a faith, the host population first loses the men themselves; and if their death unbalances the sex ratio, the losses can include the reproductive costs of women left unmated. The battle casualties also threaten the well-being of war widows and their children. Islam limits these secondary losses by allowing each man to have up to four wives. This keeps the women fed and bearing children while saving youngsters from orphanhood. Since dying for Islam only spreads the faith when the captured population outnumbers losses in the capturing population, the polygyny meme can play a crucial role. The faith again commands its own propagation—both by urging the gains and by limiting the losses.

Men are also more willing to take on the risks of military jihad when they know that both wife and children can survive their deaths, and the wives object less stridently too. If this makes Muslims better warriors, then it likewise helps the faith spread by jihad.

Polygyny and Ample Brotherhood

In parts of the world lacking formal safety nets, polygyny also acts as a kind of primitive life insurance for women during peacetime. If widowed, a young mother can transfer to her brother-in-law as an add-on wife with add-on children. Because he is already the children's uncle, he is more willing to take custody as their stepfather and provider.

Aside from aiding survival, the system can also raise the number of births per woman through an indirect route: First, it causes single women and their parents to favor those suitors who have brothers—the more, the better. This in turn causes the parents of one boy to prefer having additional sons, so that none should have trouble attracting a wife later on. But couples must typically have *four children* to have at least two sons, promoting the extremely high fertility rate of the Islamic population.

The Islamic belief in excluding women from most lucrative economic activity helps intensify their need for "brother-in-law insurance," as their unemployability threatens women with graver consequences should they ever end up with no husband at all. That, in turn, raises their need to spurn the brotherless suitor and further encourages any boy's parents to try for multiple sons. The severely restricted role of Muslim women thus contributes to the religion's propensity toward high birth rates, explaining why natural selection favors more restrictions on Muslim women than on women of other faiths.

The high Muslim birth rate, along with high conversion rates in some areas, makes Islam the world's fastest growing religion in absolute numbers.

MORMONISM

Mormonism forms its own scripturally distinct minibranch of the Judeo-Christian-Islamic family tree. Doubling in population every twenty years, its rapid growth results from combining high fertility with vigorous proselytism.

Mormon proselytic drives resemble those of other Christians, except that young adult Mormons spend two years each as missionaries. Concentrating the effort in their young adult years helps them reach impressionable young adult audiences. Young adults also make better "prizes" as converts because their children subsequently grow up Mormon.

A distinctively Mormon meme also boosts their reproduction levels beyond those of typical North American Christians. That meme says God created all human souls long ago, forcing them to wait in a preborn state for earthly humans to liberate them through birth. This makes Mormons feel that their own reproduction does a great favor for those unborn souls, especially given the divine advantages of being born Mormon. The parents of course raise all those deliberately numerous children in the Mormon faith, achieving a new mechanism of parental expansion.

HUTTERITES

The Hutterite family achieves an average reproduction rate exceeding *ten* children per couple, perhaps the highest faith-driven fecundity rate in North America. Superficially, Hutterites resemble the Amish in their old-fashioned attire and agrarian life-style, as documented by John Hostetler in *Hutterite Society*. They also host many common Christian memes, including monogamous marriage norms. The biggest memetic difference concerns family structure: hosts live in colonies where all adults share the parental responsibility for each child. Children must develop no closer ties with their biological parents than with other adults.

By distributing parental responsibility, the Hutterites greatly dilute the usual pragmatic motives for regulating fertility. Having one more child only slightly raises a couple's expected share of care and support efforts. This, then, accounts for their extraordinary achievements in reproduction.

Hutterites command little public attention as their numbers, though growing fast in relative terms, have only recently exceeded twenty thousand. Their life in remote areas also keeps them out of public view. Isolation insulates them from conversion to more prevalent life-styles, giving the faith a preservational advantage. This resulting low dropout rate (under 10 percent) allows the high fertility to yield rapid net expansion.

JEHOVAH'S WITNESSES

Their name alone somehow suggests that the Jehovah's Witnesses' unique expansion achievement is proselytic. The faith states that most believers will only enjoy heaven on earth—and this only after believers proclaim their faith throughout the world. Adherents therefore spread the faith to hasten their arrival in earthly heaven.

Jehovah's Witnesses also believe in social and cultural separatism from the "worldly" populace of non-Witnesses, while still sharing the same cities and towns with them. The separatism can involve restricting friendships to other Witnesses, or shunning common cultural practices such as wearing Halloween costumes or reciting the U.S. Pledge of Allegiance.

These barriers to involvement with non-Witnesses block "worldly" people from exerting strong influence on the believer, thus preserving the faith. Yet the barriers also provide added incentive to proselytize: a Jehovah's Witness who desires friendship with an outsider must first act to convert him.

A taboo against college education, on the other hand, reduces the Jehovah's Witnesses' ability to find converts on campus the way other movements do. Yet the taboo helps the faith retain converts found elsewhere by depriving them of mental tools that can lead to questioning and discarding the faith. This gives the college taboo preservational fitness to offset its proselytic cost. By allowing young couples to end schooling and start having children sooner, the taboo can also increase family size. This adds parental advantage to the taboo's profile, helping spread the faith as well.

A distinctive cluster of memes thus make the Jehovah's Witnesses, founded in 1872, a familiar and expanding feature of the religious world.

SHAKERS

Natural selection ensures that only the most contagious religions succeed in winning large and durable host populations. In the important "other side" of the process, extinction befalls religions with feeble contagion profiles.

The Shaker movement started with extreme proselytic zeal, yet it also strongly promoted celibacy among its members. Celibacy probably boosted proselytic activity by giving adherents more time and mobility for proselytizing, but virtually eliminated parental transmission. Eventually, the missionary efforts reached their saturation point—the point when all non-hosts amenable to conversion had already been converted. The American Shaker population peaked at about six thousand in the mid-1800s, but from that time on, the faith suffered a gradual, childless decline toward extinction. Such removal of "non-vigorous" religion from the ideosphere contributes to the broader selection process, ensuring the survival "fitness" of those faiths that remain.

RELIGION AND SCIENCE REVISITED

Numerous thinkers have suggested that modern scientific knowledge would push *all* religion toward extinction. Yet old religions continue to defy such forecasts. Moreover, new and vigorous religious movements continually form. Many once thought that the theory of evolution by natural selection would spell the end of religious myths. Yet the very phenomenon of evolution by natural selection easily propels religions past the minor challenges raised by scientific ideas. Even evolutionism loses popular ground to divine creationism in modern times.

Memetic analysis of religion illuminates a stark contrast between religious and scientific thought: religious thought generally holds that certain special beliefs are divinely created. Memetic science contends that great religions evolve from a vast accumulation of observable, mundane human actions. The creation–evolution conflict thus opens a new front: the origin of religions.

6

PRESCRIPTION BELIEFS: THOUGHT CONTAGIONS AND HEALTH

To die for an idea is to place a pretty high price upon conjectures.
—ANATOLE FRANCE

A talk show host gives testimonials to a new diet. A man tells his sick friend about the healing power of a mineral tablet. A psychotherapist analyzes a colleague's departures from orthodox theory. Most people encounter health beliefs espoused with religious zeal—and not just from faith healers. Whether true, false, or somewhere in between, the beliefs often propagate for reasons having little to do with medical reality.

CIRCUMCISION

Though widely considered a health practice today, circumcision has an even longer religious history. Hebrews practiced it thousands of years ago on their male offspring. It then transferred to early Christians, who continued the practice while abandoning many other Jewish customs. So arguably, circumcision owes much of its prevalence to an accident of religious history—by flourishing in the parent faith of fast-spreading Christianity. The question thus shifts to why circumcision propagated in ancient Jews, despite the risks of primitive surgery.

Disease weighs in as a modern-day explanation for the ancient practice, though the preventive value of circumcision remains controversial. Certain viruses, notably the AIDS virus, may infect uncircumcised men more readily. If similar viruses afflicted the ancient world, then the circumcised would hold the advantage at surviving long enough to pass on their customs. Yet an intact foreskin gives natural defense against other microorganisms, casting doubt on which way the advantage should run. The doubt strengthens from postsurgical infection risk in primitive conditions. Finally, if pagans were more promiscuous than Jews, then any anti-infective practice should have spread fastest in pagans—another blow to the disease theory of circumcision.

Instead, circumcision may have spread by raising reproductive rates. Circumcision eliminates the self-gliding capacity of the penis, channeling more lust to vaginal intercourse by limiting nonlubricated arousal methods. Activities ranging from masturbation to nearly vaginal sex become more difficult without an applied lubricant. In ancient times, the need for extra lubricants could have posed some challenge, leading couples to just go ahead and do it vaginally. The circumcision meme would therefore have flourished parentally.

In modern times, the wider availability of lubricants reduces the reproductive advantage of the circumcision meme. Yet even the mild inconvenience of needing a lubricant can favor intercourse during the heat of passion. And modern surgery is safer and easier, helping circumcision continue its long history.

BOTTLE-FEEDING

On the female side, fertility differences exert their influence on the culture of infant feeding. The most old-fashioned method keeps babies at their mothers' breast day and night, where they feed at an average interval of six minutes. Done this way, breast-feeding has a natural contraceptive effect: the frequently nursing mother does not ovulate until the baby is weaned a few years later. The biological mechanism provides birth spacing needed to prevent babies from starving under primitive conditions.

Memes that shorten natural birth-spacing can proliferate parentally in times and places where women have extra food for infants. Some of these memes act by changing breast-feeding schedules to the point of diminished contraceptive effect; others lead women to dispense with breast-feeding altogether.

Cultural mores relegating breasts and breast-feeding to strict privacy might replicate in part by making mothers alter their breast-feeding schedules. In cultural groups holding these memes, women cannot easily breast-feed every six minutes day and night. They must consolidate their feedings into several larger feedings per day. But this disrupts the hormonal mechanism behind breast-feeding's contraceptive effects, raising reproductive rates for cultures that hide their breast-feeding. In settings with enough nutrition to make the extra births viable, the extra babies survive long enough to learn breast-privacy memes from their parents. Breast-privacy memes can thereby gain enough propagation to augment their prevalence in wealthier parts of the world. Of course, other reasons exist for covered-breast memes, as they fit into a broader system of nudity taboos.

As a more radical departure from frequent breast-feeding, the idea of bottle-feeding can also enlarge family size. Mothers who bottle-feed their babies resume ovulation even sooner than those who consolidate breast-feeding for privacy. Yet safe and effective bottle formulas only became widely available in the twentieth century. That leaves bottle-feeding memes too few generations of parental replication to account for their prevalence by midcentury. Instead, the old breast-privacy memes provided the real impetus for switching to bottles once they became safe. The bottle offered women the convenience of keeping their breasts covered and babies fed without frequent trips to a private room.

More recently, the bottle's popularity has declined as a result of second thoughts about the health advantages of breast-feeding. Most mothers simply value their babies' health over personal convenience. Yet die-hard bottle feeders could still hold enough reproductive edge to regain the majority generations from now.

DIETS

Thought contagions play a more ironic role in weight-loss diets. The most satisfying result sought by most dieters is permanent reduction to a target weight range. But commercial diets can reap more profit from long-term *repeat* customers, giving companies an interest in eventually failing to keep the pounds off. Moreover, schemes that repeatedly reach temporary results can achieve better meme replication.

People on a crash reduction diet usually become preoccupied with the diet and the memes behind it. This alone leads them to express the memes frequently during the diet episode. They also express their diet memes to elicit cooperation of others during social meals. The diet meme thus enjoys more proselytic replication during its activated phase than during quiescent, nondieting phases. So the more often adherents diet, the more often they retransmit the memes. By *failing* to change long-term habits, a dietary meme set can actually induce those episodes of recurrent dieting—and recurrent meme dissemination. The "defective" memes thereby grab a proselytic edge over more permanent weight-control methods.

Diet schemes also differ in how often they induce inquiries from nonhosts. Each time adherents achieve dramatic weight loss, virtually all their regular acquaintances notice. Many—especially the overweight—go on to ask, "How did you do it?" and the newly thin usually answer by retransmitting their diet memes. The replication advantage here depends on how well the diet memes lead to drastic weight loss. But unless dieters go back to recurrent dieting, their acquaintances eventually stop marveling and inquiring. New acquaintances replace old, and lasting acquaintances eventually forget about long-lost obesity. So as before, optimal meme replication benefits from "programmed" recurrences of obesity and dieting. The more a diet system causes drastic loss and regaining cycles, the better it spreads by word of mouth. So the diets *depend* on pathological aspects for their retransmission, and that keeps diet pathologies prevalent.

FREUDIAN PSYCHOANALYSIS

Sometimes described as a cultural movement or a secular religion, Freudian psychoanalysis propagates itself by commanding adherents to long-term involvement. With a course of therapy typically running for decades, the Freudian system supports a larger therapist population than briefer alternatives can. Even if a briefer therapy gives better results, a Freudian practice with the same number of clients entails more therapy sessions. This forces the population of Freudian psychologists to educate more clinical practitioners, vigorously propagating the meme set. Although some may feign belief to gain business advantage, they cannot freely propagate plans for disingenuous practice without ruining their own businesses. That gives the replication advantage to sincere Freudians, since the sincere practice likewise thrives on long-term clients.

Freudian theory also gives adherents a systematic way of dispensing with contrary opinions. When someone asserts that Freud was wrong, the adherent can turn to Freud's theory of defense mechanisms to label the contrary ideas as neurotic repressions, or denials of truth. The Freudian thus mounts an immune reaction to the contrary memes, preserving the Freudian memes for future propagation.

When Freudians voice their analytic reactions to unbelievers, it also pressures those unbelievers toward either changing their minds or becoming silent on the subject. Few, after all, want to be seen as neurotic or delusional. Freudian memes thus help their own propagation while suppressing propagation for contrary theories.

So whether flawed or not, Freud's insights into the individual psyche ultimately ride the unconscious dynamics of population psychology.

ASTROLOGY

Whereas Freudians trace mental health back to childhood, astrologers make truly bold claims, tracing all matters of health and well-being back to the moment of birth. Though the idea predates modern science, today's astrologers often try to put a scientific spin on their methods, as with assertions that heavenly bodies affect personality by way of gravity.

As with any doctrine, paid practitioners of astrology have fiscal motives for spreading the memes. Yet much of astrology's professional and grass-roots replication is due to its built-in triggers for trust and perennial proselytism.

People who believe in astrology often try to give their friends and family the benefit of the "knowledge" by sharing astrological advice and forecasts. So they expose others to astrological memes. Once received, the memes benefit from the proponent's good intentions: with "helpful" advice mostly offered to friends and family, the astrological messenger generally occupies a position of trust to the listener. As family and friends, listeners can also form a captive audience, especially to a "helpful" message. Even those listeners who do not know the adherent well can still find that the "helpful" structure of astrological messages engenders trust.

For all of this, most listeners still do not convert from just a single memetic exposure. Astrology memes give themselves a path around this problem each time the astrological "signs" change. With each change of signs, the adherent finds new and sincere reasons for sharing astrology with others. Those not adopting the memes on first exposure get numerous additional exposures.

Though the underlying suggestion to become an astrological believer remains constant, the specific forecasts keep changing. That makes subsequent proselytism sound just different enough to prevent blanket rejections from many listeners. Any skepticism raised by one horoscope need not apply to a subsequent forecast, since the specific content differs. Nor do listeners just shut out the message by saying, "I've heard it before." They keep listening, often to the point that the basic beliefs sink in. By their very structure, astrological memes keep the proselytism flowing and the ears listening. Belief spreads from the time-honored impact of repeating a message over and over, giving astrology an enviable following.

MEMES AND AIDS

Some sexually transmitted diseases originated recently enough to let human memetics affect the course of viral evolution. The AIDS virus, in particular, shows signs of genetic adaptation to an environment governed by human sexual memes. With theories of a recent monkey origin of AIDS now discounted, a strong theory must consider how HIV evolved in humans—specifically, in its early decades of heterosexual transmission in Africa.

Other sexually transmitted diseases guided the basic development of HIV as an immune-suppressing virus. By suppressing immunity, HIV realized an opportunity to spread itself by bringing other STDs out of remission and helping them spread. The other diseases, once spread, created open sores in new people. HIV then used these sores on sex partners as ports for entering new victims. The virus evolved to help itself by fostering and "using" other contagions.

HIV also evolved ways of helping and using thought contagions.

The old sub-Saharan clan, with its sexually open relationships, offers a way for viruses to manipulate sexual behavior to suit viral transmission. To promote its own propagation, a virus need only cause people to change sex partners more often. Virulence does just that by making people recurrently lose all their sex partners. Re-activating old STDs helps in this regard, but in the developing world, STD alone seldom provokes the sexual quarantine typical in wealthier settings. Instead, it takes a greater virulence, the kind that sickens to the point of sexual disability. By rescrambling sexual relationships, the more severe viral strains thus outpropagated the milder strains during the evolution of HIV.

Faster-propagating HIV strains could also more easily "afford" the loss of long-infected victims. Viruses normally lose propagation when they kill their hosts. Yet with fast contagion, those infected ten years earlier represent a small fraction of the total infected. So when virulence helps a virus spread faster, it can more than make up for the loss of old victims by accumulating new victims.

Virulent HIV can even stir up promiscuity in people who normally practice prolonged monogamy. When one partner carries a virus from a previous mate, the current partner gets it too. If the strain is mild, the couple can stay together, possibly living out their lives without further spreading the virus. But if the strain is harsh, one of the partners eventually has symptoms sufficiently terrifying to scare off the mate. With a long latency period, the mate who runs often remains healthy long enough to find a new partner. Meanwhile, the sicker mate experiences several episodes of remission, allowing him to likewise expose new partners. Virulence, long latency, and multiple remissions form a diabolical replication mode allowing the virus to invade nearly monogamous segments of a population.

HIV actually enhanced this ability to shatter human relationships by establishing a bad reputation. Once the virus spawned thought contagions about "slim disease" in African communities, people knew ahead of time that a sickening mate was doomed. That, in turn, hastened healthier but infected mates' decisions to run away. As with biological contagions, HIV evolved ways of spreading the thought contagions that helped spread HIV.

High-incidence areas also attained bad reputations, even early on. Knowing nothing of the virus, people in badly hit villages would spread the idea that a rival village had placed a curse on them. As the latently infected fled from these terrifying places, they carried the virus into low-incidence areas, helping it spread faster. So the cruelest HIV strains spawn thought contagions that hasten viral propagation. Cruel strains thereby outpropagate the mild strains in humans, precisely because of our species' capacity for thought, communication, and rumor.

The mutually amplifying spread of HIV with other STDs meets stiff resistance in developed countries, where most STDs receive effective treatment. So a virus that spreads rampantly in African heterosexuals remains less rampant in the heterosexuals of richer countries. Those who can afford it often react to syphilis, chancroid, and herpes by suspending sex and starting aggressive treatment, slowing the vaginal spread of HIV in the developed countries. Those countries also slow HIV transmission with common use of condoms, spermicides, diaphragms, and circumcision dating back to before the discovery of AIDS. But in "underdeveloped" subgroups such as runaway teens and the poor, coital HIV transmission stays on a fast track even in rich countries.

In its early years in the developed world, HIV spread fastest in the population of males who performed both insertive and receptive anal sex. With anal sex, the virus spreads most efficiently from insertive to receptive partners, even without other STDs. So recursive transmission largely depended on those who played *both roles,* while their receptive-only partners (male and female) suffered mostly nonrecursive infections. The virus thus capitalized on promiscuity and anal sex memes among homosexual men, though it did not help spawn those memes.

For American gays, the features that HIV evolved back in Africa still helped the virus manipulate its way through populations, as it again spread in part by shattering relationships. Moreover, it again manipulated the infected by way of rumor: once a particular bar, bathhouse, or city developed a bad reputation for AIDS, people would migrate to bars, bathhouses, or cities with fewer known cases, spreading HIV to more settings. The virus had carried its ability to stir synergistic thought contagions to a new continent.

Among exclusively gay male populations, natural selection no longer favored high efficiency in vaginal transmission. Gay male to female back to gay male transmission would have mattered little in this part of the epidemic, and the strains evolving mostly in gay men would show faded levels of vaginal contagiousness. That would account for still more of the prevalence difference between male and female or homosexual and heterosexual sectors. Yet at least one strain, the "E" strain, evolved in the opposite direction, becoming highly contagious by vaginal intercourse. Though still uncommon in North America and Europe, its spread could change the demographics of AIDS in these regions.

After scientists identified AIDS in the United States, new sexually transmitted beliefs sprang up almost instantly. Beliefs of the general form "not me, not my kind" proliferated through high-, medium-, and low-risk communities, as did beliefs that the disease does not even spread sexually. Naturally, the memes enjoyed emotional appeal. Yet they also spread proselytically, from adherents trying to convince potential partners that sex posed little danger.

In the gay population, those assertions took forms such as "Sex doesn't cause AIDS," and "It's not a gay disease," which spread widely in the early 1980s. These memes helped HIV continue spreading among gay men.

Mainstream morality compounded the trouble for gays. Health warnings against promiscuity, unprotected sex, and anal sex triggered widespread "immune reactions." Even from well-intentioned sources, many gays perceived the messages as resembling the gay-taboo memes they had already rejected. Such cross-reacting memetic immunity gave HIV enough transmission time to achieve some of the world's highest infection rates in large gay neighborhoods. People often resisted converting to monogamous safe sex until after witnessing the epidemic firsthand—too late to stop a slow-acting virus.

Once most gays knew an HIV victim, the safe monogamy memes picked up tremendous proselytic drive. People spread the memes to current or potential partners in order to save both their own and their partner's lives. They also spread the memes to save friends and loved ones who were not prospective partners. Once prevalent, the new memes finally brought the rate of new infections in gay men down to a mere trickle.

Meanwhile, public health warnings spread the fear of AIDS among heterosexuals, making heterosexual sex likewise contingent on convincing potential partners of its safety. So the idea "It's not a heterosexual disease" spread widely by the late 1980s, giving the virus more propagation time in parts of the heterosexual population as well.

In most animals, viruses generally lose propagation when they kill their own hosts. Yet in humans, thought contagions give viruses a unique set of obstacles and manipulation potentials that favor virulent strains of sexually transmitted disease. This may well explain why STDs strike our own species so harshly.

CONTAGIOUS CURES

What we do *after* we get sick admits of further thought contagions. Though many contagious cures hold scientific merit, others do not, flourishing instead on pure infectiousness. These "prescription beliefs" often spread centrally, from the merchants and advertisers who stand to make money from them. Yet "cures" for everything from hiccoughs to AIDS also spread on a grass-roots level, where they evolve by natural selection.

When people try a treatment prescribed by a friend, they often experience what scientists call the *placebo effect:* inert pills called *placebos* make people "feel better" if they are falsely labeled as curative drugs. People who experience strong placebo effects from a particular "remedy" swear by it just as surely as if the cure were totally real. When they find friends and relatives with similar ailments, they usually pass the memes along to them, too. The motives for doing so range from altruism and the desire to be owed a favor to more selfish motives such as "protecting" oneself from other people's germs by trying to cure them. Beliefs in cure-all powers of vitamins, herbs, bee pollens, and other substances often spread this way.

Homeopathic "remedies" achieve thought contagion by manipulating believers more actively. Invented nearly two centuries ago, the homeopathic school of treatment still flourishes in the realm known as "alternative medicine."

The basic homeopathy meme calls for drugs producing the same symptoms as the disease being treated. An additional homeopathy meme asserts the counterintuitive claim that the more dilute the drug, the higher its potency. A third meme recommends starting at low "potency" (higher concentration) before "escalating" the treatment with higher "potency" (lower drug concentration).

These three tenets lead people to *think* they have proved the validity of homeopathy when in fact they have merely proved its ability to confuse. When people use a homeopathic drug on a trial basis, the drug can indeed produce symptoms similar to those of the illness under treatment. Naturally, this makes them feel worse. So they try the "higher potency" of a more dilute mixture. The more dilute mixture in reality produces fewer symptoms, and patients feel better. The confused patients thus "confirm" a victory for homeopathy. The experience converts them to believers, rather than just skeptical experimenters. Thus convinced, they usually go about retransmitting homeopathic suggestions to other ailing people.

Homeopathic memes do, however, lose adherents when used to treat serious diseases such as streptococcus infections, heart disease, and even AIDS. The memes also face stiff competition from conventional medicine. In spite of this, homeopathy still replicates enough to maintain a persistent minority following.

EXERCISE AND SPORT

Backed by modern scientific studies, believers in discretionary exercise spread their beliefs for some of the same reasons people spread beliefs in a disease remedy: to help friends and family. People also feel motivated to spread exercise memes to their mates for sexual and aesthetic reasons, hoping to boost their physical attractiveness. Yet long before its proliferation for health and fitness, discretionary exercise proliferated in the form of sport. Here, too, thought contagion and natural selection play a part.

The obvious factor spreading any new sport is fun. If this were the sole factor involved, then the most widespread sports would simply be the most fun sports.

Yet the *structure* of a sport also affects its proliferation by affecting its need for recruitment. If a sport is hard to play without two teams of nine players, its enthusiasts must recruit and educate new people. That happens often among boys, who readily find and persuade their peers. When the boys grow up, they teach the sport to their sons, adding parental transmission to proselytism. Thus, knowledge of how to play baseball spread throughout the United States within a mere century of the first games. Other team sports follow the pattern, giving the country its fervent emphasis on big team sports.

STREET GANGS

The kind of team recruitment that favors boyhood sports on the one hand can proliferate street gangs on the other, typically harming public health through violence and drugs. Rival gangs, like opposing teams, need to acquire new members to stay in the game. The gang members all know this and pressure nonmembers to join. Yet their recruitment motives go well beyond those of winning or losing a ball game: members want to expand their own gang to control more turf and revenue. They even recruit to save their own lives during gang wars, both by putting the new member on their side and by keeping him or her off the enemy side. Gangs with the most hostile and criminal attitudes can thus have the most intense recruitment needs, causing them to outpropagate milder gangs. They also use severe pressure, such as offering "protection" to the prospective recruit—a deal one can hardly refuse. Propelled by such life-and-death motives in both recruiters and their targets, street gang memes replicate tenaciously despite community efforts to stop them.

Communities do, however, achieve different levels of immunity to street gang memes. Families with fathers present afford perhaps the strongest immunity to gang memes. First, fathers give their offspring considerable pressures contrary to the pressure for joining a gang. Second, fathers, more than mothers, can usually give their sons and daughters physical protection independent of what the gangs promise. With fathers present throughout a neighborhood, the gang immunity amplifies itself. Youths become both resistant to gangs and less likely to encounter them since other youths also resist recruitment. In that respect, fathers do for gang memes what vaccines do for viruses: even fatherless teenagers have less gang involvement in a community with mainly present fathers, for much the same reason that an unvaccinated child does better living in a vaccinated population.

DRUG ABUSE

Public discourse often describes drug abuse as an epidemic, too. Though not exactly a contagion of thought, the addiction to a specific drug can become a replicating brain condition, and hence, a meme. The condition spreads in two stages: First, an addict transmits the *idea* of using the drug recreationally, often just by letting others see its consumption. Second, those who adopt and act on a recreational consumption meme often go on to become addicts themselves. When they do, they join in frequently retransmitting the recreational-use meme. Mixed with the two-stage contagion is the one-stage transmission of recreational drug memes from those who escape full addiction. (See figure 3.)

Naturally, those who sell drugs devote much effort to spreading prodrug memes. Yet the drugs often contribute an

FIGURE 3

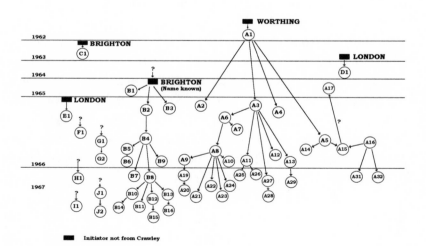

The Spread of Heroin Abuse Among 58 Young People Living in the Town of Crawley, near London, in 1967. Such epidemiological charts work well for memetic contagions, including drug abuse. *Source:* R. de Alarcon, "The Spread of Heroin Abuse in a Community," *Community Health* 1, no. 3. (1969).

element of self-promotion: the more intensely addictive, the more preservational advantage the memes enjoy. Addiction fosters proliferation both by retaining people longer and by making them retransmit the drug use ideas for additional years. The phenomenon spreads all kinds of addictive drugs, from tobacco and alcohol to heroin and cocaine.

After drug addictions spread through a population, natural selection begins acting against the drug memes. Addicts die off in greater numbers than nonaddicts, and declining health damages their ability to inspire imitation by others. Meanwhile, those with strong taboos against recreational drugs retain better mental functioning, making them more effective at spreading their opinions through child raising and proselytism. This replication advantage only becomes significant after many of those who lack drug taboos actually succumb to drug problems.

Hosts of drug taboos also feel motivated to spread the word against drugs, since they regard it as a matter of saving others from destruction. Here, too, the motivation and the replication increase during times of prevalent drug abuse.

With taboos spreading most vigorously after drug abuse becomes prevalent, society could thus face continuing cycles of waxing and waning drug consumption. Yet in the future, drugs for escaping reality face increasing competition from new drugs for adapting to reality.

SMART PILLS

The newest class of psychoactive drugs are those that enhance memory and intellectual performance: the *nootropics*. Their putative benefits include better and faster learning, better recall, and enhanced or accelerated thinking. Most of today's versions may work as stimulants, but researchers are pursuing more potent and far-reaching drugs.

The idea of using nootropic drugs has just begun to propagate. One can only speculate on where it will lead, but if the drugs work as advertised, they raise the prospects for some amusing replication forces.

At first, the pronootropic meme would gain hosts by way of classical imitation—that is, through motivational replication. Potentially vast numbers of people might accept nootropic use as fast as they heard of it to gain educational and career advantage. Yet others would take exception for reasons ranging from religion and morality to social compliance and fear of the unnatural.

After most people hear about nootropics, the population would mostly fall into the camps of those for and those against using the drugs. At this point, a true replicator contest would ensue.

Those who use nootropics would presumably retain their memes longer than those who memetically reject the drugs. In particular, they would remember their reasons for using nootropic drugs longer than those opposed to nootropics would remember *their* reasons. During most of life, these differences would remain slight. Yet advancing age would produce increasing differences between the two groups. The pronootropic meme can thus enjoy preservational propagation advantage: longer meme retention would boost prevalence both directly and by the extra retransmissions that lasting adherents achieve.

Drugs that enhance recall and thinking skills could incidentally enhance meme transmission *skills* as well. The drugs could, for instance, help people voice opinions more articulately and persuade a higher fraction of listeners. The drugs might even raise the quantity of opinion expressed if quick-thinking drug users simply had more thoughts on their minds each day. Either way, the effect would boost replication of the pronootropic meme but not the antinootropic meme.

Still, many nootropic users might hold back on spreading the word for competitive reasons. Being the only mentally enhanced person in a job or social setting could have its advantages. Moreover, people would want to hide the fact that some of their mental performance derived from using a drug, preferring instead to let others attribute it to natural brilliance. So even if they expressed most opinions more articulately, competitive reticence could slow the pronootropic meme enough to leave the contrary attitudes anywhere from prevalent to predominant.

Wherever competition gave way to cooperation, the incentive would favor respreading the nootropic meme. Adherents might spread the meme to family, good friends, business partners, and perhaps workplace subordinates—even if they kept it secret from others. The desire to compete more effectively against outsiders can play a part here. On the large scale, some might share nootropic knowledge with compatriots to keep the nation competitive in the world community. All of this could partly restore the replication advantage that nootropics would confer through fast and articulate thinking. Yet even in cooperative relationships, many would not trust their own medical judgment well enough to freely recommend drugs to others. The memes would spread, but not wildly.

If those taking nootropic drugs do indeed achieve more upward mobility, their numbers will gradually swell in the upper middle and higher classes. People striving to imitate the successful would then start adopting pronootropic memes in greater numbers.

Still, those with moral taboos would seldom convert, even with images of success dangling before them. The Mormons and other fundamentalist groups might lead the resistance, keeping the memetic contest alive for generations.

As the generations pass, any differences in parent-to-child transmission would increasingly figure into the course of this contest.

Parents who give enhanced learning drugs to their children could hold the most obvious advantage in meme transmission: their children can better learn what parents teach, including what they teach about nootropic drugs. Yet they could also become better able to question their parents' teachings, leading to some replication losses for pronootropic memes.

Those using nootropics might also have better luck at earning enough money to attract a mate and start a family. This could in principle lead the nootropic movement to have more children, thus replicating faster.

In reality, the trend could run the other way. If nootropics users achieve more education and analytical skill, they might frequently reject traditional and zealous religions. That in turn could lower both their proselytic zeal and their reproductive output. Those who memetically reject the nootropics would then raise more children and do more proselytizing—possibly enough to outpopopulate the believers in nootropics, or at least enough to challenge them far into the future. So Daniel Keyes's story of *Flowers for Algernon* might come true on the scale of population memetics.

The memetics of psychotropic drugs may evoke Aldous Huxley's *Brave New World,* but the memetics of cloning does even better.

MEMETIC CLONES

Normally considered the stuff of science fiction, human cloning would certainly raise moral hackles if it ever really happened. Yet those who accept the practice may end up raising more children than those who reject it. Procloning couples might typically have *four children:* two conjugal offspring and two clones. And the cloned offspring would typically feel very inclined to copy procloning memes from their parents. After enough generations, social stigmas could well shift from those who have clones to those remaining cloneless. Society would memetically change its mind on cloning.

A GERM THEORY OF IDEAS

Well over a century ago, the understanding of health and disease advanced with a new theory that infectious agents called *germs* often play important roles. Though the theory never engulfed *all* of medicine, the science has advanced enormously, studying germs that range from deadly to beneficial. The theory of evolution has furthered the revolution by helping science predict how and why contagions act as they do.

With memetics arises a *germ theory of ideas,* concerning all areas of life, including health. Though the theory is still new, it too can eventually grow into a mature discipline in its own right and advance our understanding of the human condition.

7

CONTROVERSY:
THOUGHT CONTAGIONS
IN CONFLICT

War is a contagion.
—FRANKLIN D. ROOSEVELT

Some of the liveliest thought
contagions live outside the strict headings of family, sex, religion, and health. These include memes on abortion, war, handguns, and other public issues. The tendency to ignite controversy unites these "leftover" thought contagions. Competing
beliefs in these areas move their adherents deeply, sometimes to
risk everything in spreading or stopping an idea.

CONTROVERSIAL RADIO

With talk radio, controversy becomes an attention-getting device; the stations seek shows that get a maximum crowd listening and hearing the commercials. Yet for every program that succeeds, others fail at the trial-run stage. And part of what decides a talk show's fate is whether or not it spawns thought contagions in the target population. It doesn't require memetic engineering either: a few lucky announcers and producers can hit a contagious formula by accident, and other stations buy into their success by syndication.

A *predictably* opinionated talk show serves as a vehicle of belief transfer from dedicated listeners, much as scripture functions to the followers of a religion. Taking in the talk show, however, requires much less effort than reading a book. The talk shows can also cost virtually no time to absorb if they air during the workday. To proselytize, you don't need to bend someone's ear for half an hour and ask them to spend long hours reading; just tell them to tune in.

The midday broadcasts also offer a more passive way to proselytize: merely tune in daily within earshot of the unconverted, and wait for the message to sink in. This form of proselytism can reach several listeners at once and hit them with better oratory than the average believer can muster. It also eludes much of the antiproselytism immunity that comes with one-to-one persuasion: superficially, it appears that the believer is just listening to the radio and not trying to persuade anyone. Such a "mere listener" doesn't hear "Shut up!" as often as an overt proselytizer would, just an occasional "Turn it off!" from someone who comes off looking like a closed-minded censor.

A lesser technology, radio holds its own against television when it comes to ideological broadcasts. Unlike television, which only reaches those who want to watch, radio programs can penetrate the minds of those who do not care to listen. The average radio is also cheap and portable enough for people to carry to places such as work and expose new people to the user's favorite show. Most televisions do not travel, and those that do can barely serve one viewer at a time—hardly a means for proselytizing. So natural selection currently gives radio a strong role in meme propagation.

Content also matters in the replication game. The most widely heard show of the 1990s, Rush Limbaugh's, practically calls out for replicator theory by describing its believers as "ditto-heads."

First, the show carries an urgent theme: the country must renounce all kinds of liberalism or face dire consequences. Those persuaded by the message then "realize" that they must help spread the word in order to save the nation, so they deploy their radios and voices accordingly.

Second, Limbaugh maintains an ambiguity between the serious and the jocular, allowing individual listeners to latch on to the most urgent-sounding message that *they themselves* can take seriously. This optimizes the proselytic drive across individuals with different levels and types of conservatism.

Third, Limbaugh treats his critics and skeptics to such derision and stereotyping (in pursuit of entertainment) that he socially pressures some dissenters into silence. Most people loathe to be laughed at or stereotyped, and therefore can easily keep their mouths shut instead of disputing Limbaugh's views with coworkers. With a history of implying death wishes against liberals, the show also harnesses the fear of hatred toward quelling criticism. Limbaugh himself says it's all entertainment, but dissenters don't always believe that, keeping their fears alive. Moreover, he does promote a conservative anger toward liberals and moderates—an anger they might avoid by concealing their beliefs. All these factors suppress replication of competing memes, helping the "listen to Limbaugh" meme flourish.

Finally, because of its right-wing, proestablishment message, people expect the Limbaugh show to hold more employer
tolerance for playing the radio at work than an equally strident
left-wing broadcast. As a setting where people of many persua-
sions intermingle, the workplace offers a crucial opportunity
for the converted to reach the unconverted and replicate their
memes. So the "listen to Limbaugh" meme can spread more
vigorously than memes for shows regarded as ill-tolerated by
management.

Indeed, the desire to politically flatter the management
adds one more reason for playing Limbaugh among coworkers,
but it incidentally spreads the meme to peers and bosses alike.
Meanwhile, left-wing listeners can only appease management
by using headphones, which suppress meme transmission to
coworkers.

After these mechanisms propelled the Limbaugh show to
its first success in Sacramento, other stations wanted to repeat
the phenomenon in their own local markets by broadcasting his
national show. As the "listen to Limbaugh" meme replicated in
various towns, it persuaded station managers to replicate the
replications in still more areas. With a faster-than-annual doubling rate, the "listen to Limbaugh" meme thus proliferated to
twenty million Americans.

Though Limbaugh and others sound like highly centralized meme sources, the actual replication control still rests with
a population of individuals. In this respect, it resembles the
replication of Biblical memes: the book itself comes from centralized publishers, but the idea of reading and believing it
spreads person to person as an indigenous thought contagion.

None of this replicator analysis actually evaluates talk radio
stars on the issues, though it certainly differs from how they
explain their own successes. To spread far and wide, the shows
do have to avoid *seriously* asserting anything *easily* refuted by
average listeners. Otherwise, their statements would trigger

widespread immune reactions. But this restriction leaves them enormous latitude, divorcing the question of validity from the phenomenon of thought contagion.

FIREARMS

The current U.S. controversy over handguns and other firearms arose when gun-control memes propagated widely enough to challenge older, more permissive firearm memes.

Old progun memes developed along with the weapons themselves, especially for military and hunting use. Guns also proliferated for private self-defense, at first from attack by strong enemies lacking firearms. After that, the demand for private guns stemmed largely from the knowledge that if others had them, then those who didn't lived in peril—especially before modern law enforcement. Progun memes thus replicated by creating a tacit threat to nonhosts, motivating them to convert.

In the United States, the belief in bearing and using arms also proliferated parentally in times of frontier expansion. Those who believed in using firearms to settle Native American lands often wound up with large plots to clear and farm. The task was labor-intensive and children were the principal source of cheap labor. So the belief in using arms to take and hold land led to more children, outpopulating more pacifist movements such as the Quakers. The Quakers, who were common in colonial times, respected American natives and their claims to territory. Yet with frontier expansion complete, the Quakers now constitute less than one American in a thousand—partly from their mild-firearm memes.

The explosion of modern handgun violence gave proselytic advantage to beliefs in gun control, as especially in people who refuse to counter the guns of others with guns of their own. Instead, the unarmed often wish to limit the threat from others by restricting access to guns. Their motives range from self-preservation and preservation of family and friends to the survival of complete strangers. Some who own guns actually share this desire for tighter gun regulations, even offering to give up their weapons if others must do the same.

To achieve the goal of gun restrictions, all these people must spread the word among voters. The feeling that their own and others' lives hang in balance intensifies the urge to proselytize. Meanwhile, the old-time reproductive advantage of progun memes has vanished, accelerating the proportionate inroads of gun-control memes. With armed land acquisition a thing of the past, the reproductive advantage may well have shifted against the progun memes. More children die playing with guns than are born to work lands taken with guns.

Yet those who feel more *protected* than threatened by gun availability have lifesaving motives for spreading *their* beliefs. Many of them proselytize to protect their investment in guns, since restrictions would lead to either gun forfeiture or difficulty in reselling the weapons. Those who like hunting, target practice, and gun collecting hasten to express progun memes too, as their pastimes might otherwise vanish.

Some of those who own guns also speak up for gun ownership as a way to deter possible transgressions from people within earshot. For them, expressing a progun meme implicitly works like the "Protected by Smith & Wesson" bumper stickers on cars, except more broadly. It serves notice against those who might terminate their jobs, run off with their fiancées, ruin their reputations, defraud them, and so forth. The great majority of these progun advocates do not really regard murder as an option, but want to retain a means of making others feel intimidated—a means that depends on the right to bear arms. A loss of gun rights for them would weaken this ability to threaten transgressors, thus posing a perceived danger against their social standing. This inspires some of the hottest progun arguments from many who could otherwise leave constitutional law to the lawyers.

Fiercely progun memes can also intimidate hosts of gun-control memes into silence, especially when the discussion turns heated. Most antigun folks would probably assume that fiercely progun people own firearms and might use them if angered. Yet few people worry about being shot by an angry gun-control advocate. This helps preserve progun memes by stopping exposures to antigun memes. It can also deter the retransmission of antigun memes to any moderate listeners present, furthering the *relative* spread of progun memes.

People who make and sell guns have commercial reasons for spreading progun memes, adding powerful voices to the progun side. The gun-control side, however, generally lacks this kind of vested interest in a specific product. Commercially motivated proselytism therefore favors the progun side over the gun-control side.

Strong replication advantages thus work on both sides of the firearms issue in modern America, keeping the controversy alive. Yet the replication advantages only determine which side outpopulates the other, not which side wins in the political process. In politics, the side with more campaign money or more intense opinion can prevail over the side with more population. Memetic forces certainly affect the political process, but not through numbers alone.

ABORTION

In modern America, abortion ranks as mother of all controversies: it simultaneously embroils moral, religious, ethnic, civil rights, sexual, and feminist passions. Some of the fight involves vested interests visible without memetic theory: American doctors, for instance, endorsed abortion bans in the nineteenth century partly to prevent a doctorless abortion market from taking over physicians' territory. Many Protestants of that century opposed abortion for fear that a Catholic majority would result from more numerous Protestant abortions. On the other side, women of this century have advocated abortion rights to counter the inequalities sometimes "justified" by citing women's job-quitting risk in pregnancy.

Widely unknown, though, is the ancient history of abortion, with differing replication rates for those who accepted or rejected it. These replication factors add invisible forces to the historical arguments on abortion.

Risky but effective abortion came into wide use during ancient Greek and Roman times, as well as in other ancient cultures, such as the Chinese. Some of the more advanced methods included thin instruments for lancing a fetus, which leads the body to abort within twenty-four hours; leaving foreign objects in the uterus; and even abortifacient herbal drugs.

On discovery of effective abortion procedures, the knowledge probably spread like any other utilitarian innovation. People who knew about abortion and specific methods would have spread the ideas to friends and relatives. Listeners would have welcomed such memes, since they confer new power in matters of reproduction.

Yet when ancient women had abortions, they risked injury and death. This danger may explain the earliest objections to the practice. With both proabortion and antiabortion memes sprouting in the population, memetic competition followed.

The Christian idea that God created sex only for intramarital procreation gave an early boost to abortion taboos. This "procreational sex" meme, which proliferated parentally, discouraged all efforts to prevent childbirth—including abortion.

Explicit abortion taboos spread themselves through childbirth too. Christians who specifically regarded abortion as sinful outreplicated Christians with the more permissive abortion memes. Antiabortionism then helped the faith itself to out-replicate alternative faiths, until Christianity and the abortion taboo permeated Western culture.

Still, some Christians rejected abortion more strenuously than others, allowing for additional memetic evolution. Among Christians with milder antiabortion ideas, the practice continued for many centuries. That left the strongly antiabortion Christians outreplicating the ones holding milder beliefs.

Equating abortion with murder rated among the strongest of antiabortion memes. As such, it achieved vigorous parental replication. The meme also provoked proselytism: believers felt a need to spread their meme in order to save the lives of the innocent unborn.

As the strongly antiabortion memes gained prevalence, they filtered into the most powerful positions in government and clergy. Both church and state inevitably acted against abortion, leaving it widely banned by the mid-nineteenth century.

These abortion bans, however, erased much of the reproductive difference that favored the bans in the first place. The more effective the ban, the higher the rate of live births per pregnancy, even among those with permissive abortion memes. Of course, some prochoice adherents had abortions in spite of the bans. Yet the bans made the practice socially and medically riskier, as well as less convenient. So once a ban took effect, it made the prochoice side raise more children than they otherwise would have.

Abortion bans also reduced some of the desire to proselytize the belief "Abortion is murder." With the practice banned, hosts no longer felt an acute sense that lives depended on spreading the word.

With competitive birth rates restored on the prochoice side, their population began catching up with the antiabortion side. The mathematics ensures that where replication and dropout rates match, the populations converge to similar sizes.

As sexual mores changed in the twentieth century, prochoice memes gained still more through proselytism and kin persuasion. Prochoice men having extramarital sex, or perhaps intramarital sex without means of child support, wanted to retransmit the prochoice meme to their mates. Meanwhile, the women's immediate relatives wanted to discourage poorly planned births as well. So the prochoice relatives also passed memes along to sexually active single women.

Though women themselves could gain more control over their reproductive and economic destinies, they arrived surprisingly late as a major voice for abortion rights. The old procreational sex meme silenced them. Fearing that endorsing abortion rights would sound like an endorsement of sexual freedom, prochoice women often kept their beliefs to themselves until sexual attitudes changed in the late 1960s and 1970s. But eventually, the feminist movement openly adopted the abortion rights meme.

As prochoice advocates proliferated, they began filtering into places once held by the antiabortion side. Eventually, bans on abortion began falling. With the Supreme Court's 1973 *Roe* versus *Wade* decision, abortion bans fell all over the United States.

After the 1973 court decision, those believing that "Abortion is murder" again felt an acute sense that lives depended on them spreading the word and acting on it. The meme spread especially well among those who already rejected abortion as a violation of the procreational sex meme. The "murderous abortion" meme not only justified the abortion taboo, but also offered an effective way to express it in the 1960s and 1970s, when sexual morality arguments had lost favor. That made "murderous abortion" the most replicated type of abortion taboo, leading to its overwhelming prevalence among modern antiabortionists. By lifting the bans that had dampened the meme's proselytic urgency, the court's *prochoice* decision put the "prolife" movement back in a growth mode.

Because the court's ruling came during the age of television, it also led to the televised proselytism of Operation Rescue. Each time the media cover an Operation Rescue event, they broadcast the organization's name—and implicitly utter the idea "Abortion is murder."

Fiercely antiabortion and progun memes spreading in the same country ensured that, in time, the two memes would combine to form a new breed of adherents. The "violence as standard fare" meme emanating from the media combined with the other two and rendered an even deadlier thought contagion. Finally, television gave assassins special access to broadcasting beliefs, adding that extra motivation to commit crimes despite heavy penalties. Indeed, television even helped killers retransmit the idea of committing an abortion clinic assassination, leading to copycat cases. Yet assassins eventually lose their voice in the community and their ability to raise children, possibly preventing them from running rampant in the long run.

Regarding the other side, the 1973 court decision raised rates of abortion in the prochoice population. Though millions of abortions had previously happened under illicit circumstances, the availability of medically and socially safe clinics increased the fraction of pregnancies terminated. The prochoice movement actually lost some of the parental replication it held during abortion bans, giving the antiabortion meme renewed advantage in the child-raising contest. Just as abortion bans had ironically *raised* prochoice reproduction, abortion liberty has ironically *reduced* prochoice reproduction.

With a growing movement of "single-issue" antiabortionists, the antiabortion meme has again filtered into high places, including the Supreme Court. The situation has regalvanized the prochoice population with proselytism to keep the reproductive freedom they gained in 1973.

If widespread abortion bans take hold again, then restored reproduction and proselytic vigor will again shift to the prochoice side. That, in turn, will lead back to renewed abortion rights and consequent trends back to banning abortion. Because government bans apply regardless of personal credo, the memetics of abortion faces the prospect of lasting instabilities.

ABORTION, CONTRACEPTION, AND LANGUAGE BARRIERS

Languages sometimes provoke controversies between majority and minority cultures. In the United States, the issue concerns the rising prevalence of monolingual Spanish in a mainly English-speaking country. Descendants of Italians, Germans, and other past immigrant groups complain that Spanish-speaking immigrants have too many Spanish-speaking children and grandchildren, requiring the country to adapt to them rather than vice versa. This situation stems more from the unconscious memetics of religion and reproduction than from a conscious stubbornness.

Americanized Catholicism offers greater tolerance of contraception and abortion than does Hispanic Catholicism. Fully Americanized Catholics therefore have fewer children than do culturally Hispanic Catholics.

Moreover, those Hispanic Americans who learn English receive more exposure to Americanized Catholicism than do their non-English-speaking counterparts. The knowledge of English helps them attend English-speaking churches, meet more English-speaking friends, and absorb a more Americanized creed. That in turn leads to more children for Spanish-speaking Hispanics than for English-speaking Hispanics.

Since parents have enormous influence over a child's primary and even secondary language, the Spanish language can replicate more often in Hispanic Americans than does the English language. The language barriers preserve their parentally prolific Catholicism, and the memetics of language, faith, and morality help make Hispanics the fastest-growing ethnic minority in North America.

Earlier Catholic immigrants arrived back when American Catholics had very large families. Learning English for those groups made for continued fecundity, preventing their non-English speakers from outpopulating the rest. So Italians, for instance, received the language more warmly, when viewed as a population.

Moving to a world scale, ethnic rivalries and the population pressures behind them touch off a truly great memetic controversy: whether or not to wage war.

JINGOISM AND PACIFISM

The topic of war sparks a recurring controversy as furious as the struggle of life and death. As with abortion, propagating prowar and antiwar memes affect government action, and government action in turn affects those meme propagations.

War and peace follow a basic cycle of lesson learning and forgetting: in peacetime, the glory and expedience of winning can hold more attention; in wartime, the horrors often hold more attention. Each war also has its own particular stakes, which can include such matters as resources, ethnicity, political doctrines, and religion. The religious wars certainly stem from memetic currents, as discussed earlier. Yet thought contagions have started some secular wars, too.

The impetus for secular warfare often involves grass-roots jingoism, especially in democracies. Holding a belief that "We must vanquish a dangerous enemy" naturally leads adherents to proselytize, since the "we" part of the meme requires collective action. Regarding the enemy as "dangerous" makes the need to proselytize more urgent: adherents see the lives of family, neighbors, and self as potentially depending on military action. The most clearly threatening enemies thus provoke the most vigorous prowar proselytism.

To some, however, the spread of hawkish ideas poses a greater threat than "the enemy." People expected to do the actual fighting, for instance, can feel endangered enough to start spreading antiwar memes. Worried family and friends add still more voices to the antiwar side.

Yet the task of fighting mostly falls on young men, who usually do not know the horrors of war firsthand. To them, the dangers of military service can seem abstract and remote compared with dangers seen in "the enemy." That can give hawkish memes a replication advantage during peacetime. When it happens, the memetic balance tips in favor of war.

The onset of war typically shifts the replication advantages gradually back in favor of peace. The most direct change involves different mortality rates among hawks and doves. Young men with the most hawkish memes volunteer for service most often, and for the most dangerous missions once enlisted. In a very bloody war, such meme-linked volunteerism selectively depopulates the hawks, letting the doves survive in greater proportions.

Men whose memes lead them to death or to several years of foreign fighting can also have fewer children than their dovish counterparts. Single soldiers postpone marrying, and the married postpone having children. In lengthy and bloody wars, doves can thereby do more child raising and pass their memes down to more children than do hawks.

Mounting death tolls also increase antiwar proselytism. Men of draft age become much more worried as they see and hear about dying peers. Those who happen to oppose the war therefore speak out more frequently and forcefully than they did in peacetime. In a lengthy and bloody war, the proselytism can last long enough to shift public opinion back toward pacifism.

When public opinion does shift back to pacifism faster than soldiers win the war, the war can end without a military "victory." For the United States, this happened in the Vietnam War. Fast-replicating fears of the communist "enemy" in Indochina helped start the war in the first place. But once the United States entered the war, an antiwar movement sprouted and kept spreading as the war dragged on. Eventually, the antiwar memes prevailed and the United States pulled out.

In the Iran–Iraq war, the heavy death toll among Iranian "martyrs" figured almost as heavily as did antiwar proselytism. By "martyring" its most hawkish citizens, Iran unwittingly depopulated the prowar side of its society. After a military stalemate and continued "dehawking" of the population, the hardline Iranian government grudgingly accepted a cease-fire.

Even when a war ends decisively, it can still raise the prevalence of pacifism on the "winning" side. During the long and bloody First World War, American doves enjoyed greater survival and reproduction than their most hawkish compatriots. With gruesome casualty rates, people also denounced war more often, inevitably influencing the prevailing attitude. The war ended with pacifists and isolationists holding greater prevalence than before. People who avoided "unpatriotic"-sounding speech during the war then joined in spreading pacifist and isolationist memes after the war. So antiwar memes continued rising for many years after peace broke out. Even a generation later, the public strongly resisted the president's calls to fight the Nazis and Imperial Japan, joining World War II only after the attack on Pearl Harbor.

Once the attack happened, millions of Americans simultaneously inferred that "We must vanquish a dangerous enemy." This time, the idea prevailed without needing years as a thought contagion first. Germany, on the other hand, launched World War II after time and circumstances allowed the buildup of Nazi thought contagions.

Before Hitler, Germans who regarded their country as a victim of conspiring Jews or communists felt urgent drives to spread the word. By "exposing the conspiracies," they hoped to save themselves and their nation from ruin. Whenever they met someone who challenged their ideas, the conspiratorial believer could infer their listener's "complicity" in the conspiracy, thus preserving the memes against critical challenge. Finally, by alleging fantastic crimes and fantastic dangers, racial conspiracy memes "justify" their propagation by any means that work—including lies, theft, intimidation, and murder. Full-blown Nazism later potentiated the process by telling hosts that they belonged to the "master race," making them specially qualified to do whatever it took to spread their own beliefs.

Such fiercely spreading memes naturally raise their odds of propagating into a skilled leader and can make the leader more obsessed by provoking alarm. Yet Hitler showed a level of oratorical skill that seldom occurs even in very large movements. His skills mattered more because twentieth-century technology allowed him to transmit his voice to radios across the country. The Nazi memes therefore owed part of their spectacular rise to matters of chance and timing.

The Great Depression further fueled these thought contagions by creating vast numbers of unemployed. When the Nazi memes spread into these people, they could devote abundant free time to retransmission. The depression also granted a certain "plausibility" to beliefs in Germany's victim status and thoughts of doing something about it. Finally, hard times meant more people would replicate any memes that seemed to justify mass plunder of minorities such as the Jews. The prospect of gaining enough adherents to legalize this collective robbery elicited additional proselytism from those people.

Since Nazi ideology justified violence, the spreading movement intimidated ever more unbelievers into silence. Only the most courageous could voice earnest objections to such threatening factionists, even in "polite" settings. That, in turn, gave Nazism added replication advantage over alternative memes. As the Nazis gained power, many unbelievers lost their freedom and their lives. The movement had achieved the full range of hostile propagation.

Because Nazi memes combined the hostility with extreme nationalism, the Second World War arose as the product of thought contagion. The memes had grown from a national controversy to an international terror.

CONCLUSION

A vast body of research now awaits the new field of memetics. Though this book can only scratch the surface, it will, I hope, inspire deeper study of the topics covered, and new insights into topics omitted. With more researchers working in cultures around the world and gathering relevant forms of data, the new paradigm should eventually mature to the level achieved in evolutionary biology.

As one of the most powerful forces of nature, the evolution of replicating entities by natural selection extends beyond biology, having newfound importance in the origin of beliefs. Where once we had thought *our* origins above nature, we now know the humbler truth of biological evolution. Where once we had thought our beliefs and values above the laws of nature, we increasingly know them, too, as the outcomes of natural selection.

In every corner of our lives, from how we raise young to how we treat the ill, from how we seek pleasure to what we hold sacred, from how we make love to how we wage war, evolving thought contagions live with us and in us, telling us how.

EPILOGUE: THOUGHT CONTAGIONS OF *THOUGHT CONTAGION*

By now, readers looking at the new model of belief propagation may wonder, will the theory propagate by its own principles, and what if it does? The answer matters, since hopes for more intelligence at the population level depend on knowing why we collectively believe as we do. Much as mental self-awareness plays a central role in the consciousness of an individual, so must memetic self-awareness become central to a more conscious population. Without it, intense ideologies around the world will keep spiraling out of control with reckless abandon—scarcely more self-aware than the planet's weather.

But whether societies will become memetically self-aware remains far from certain. As Daniel Dennett explains in *Consciousness Explained,* "[I]n its own terms, whether or not the meme meme replicates successfully is strictly independent of its epistemological virtue; it might spread in spite of its perniciousness, or go extinct in spite of its virtue." Indeed, it might even spread in spite of its virtue or go extinct in spite of its perniciousness! Presumably, we can look to memetics itself for clues to its own propagation.

Because memetics relates to so many hotly contested

beliefs, many who read about it find reasons to mention it in their conversations. For instance, a prochoice advocate might use memetic reasoning to characterize antiabortionists as a mere replication phenomenon. Others might cite replication phenomena as reasons for changing welfare programs. Common disputes over religion, health, and sexual morals can also bring out memetic arguments.

All these cases can spread thought contagion theory to previously unexposed listeners. Moreover, those who see thought contagion theory as helpful to their causes can make efforts to spread it even with no immediate dispute at hand. Others might spread it as a kind of "antivirus" of the mind, with or without regard for favorite causes. This would include those trying to immunize friends, relatives, and coworkers "at risk" of catching an unwelcome ideology in the neighborhood. Still others will spread it for the general betterment of humanity.

Yet the more it spreads, the more memetics theory will attract unfavorable attention from people reactive against all forms of Darwinism. A desire to keep loftier views of how belief systems originated could bring further opposition. The dispute could well become personal and dirty, much as it has in the history of creationism versus evolutionism. Some of this will actually bring more converts to memetics theory, by raising awareness of it. But in the long run, this does not assure that it can outpropagate an intense opposition.

How memetics does in the long run will depend on a heretofore uncharted influence on its hosts: to the extent the theory is valid, a population of memetics adherents would have a good idea of how to expand their own numbers. On an implicit level, thought contagion theory tells its own host population, "If you want your beliefs to gain ground, you must make efforts to respread them." Thought contagion theory can thus become a uniquely self-replicating belief system, and an object for its own discourse.

Some opponents, though, will see it as a flaw that thought contagion theory could be subject to its own principles. Yet the theory does not, in general, classify replicating memes as true or false, so it avoids refuting itself even as a self-exemplifying theory.

Others might detect a tinge of circularity if memetics goes on to exemplify itself. The point would be valid if the theory were the first and *only* example of itself, but the likelihood of that appears remote. As an example of itself, thought contagion theory should merely supply itself more data for analysis and predictions.

The real conundrum arises in using thought contagion theory to predict how widely the theory itself will spread. One could work up detailed surveys to measure how often adherents replicate the theory in various modes, and then use quantitative methods to predict its future prevalence. But people informed of the prediction might replicate the theory at different rates than those who have never heard the prediction. So the analysis goes to the second stage of trying to predict the prevalence of theory and its self-forecast; then the third stage of predicting the fate of theory with forecast of theory with forecast. And so on.

The resulting infinite regression arises from thought contagion's status as a self-referential theory. The strengths and limits of self-referential systems come under scrutiny in *Gödel, Escher, Bach: An Eternal Golden Braid* by Douglas R. Hofstadter. In adapting a famous mathematical theorem by Kurt Gödel, Hofstadter argues that any consistent theory or system powerful enough to consider itself has to be incomplete. The incompleteness arises as a "formally undecidable" question, namely, "What does thought contagion theory forecast for the contagion of thought contagion theory?" An important question with weighty implications for humanity, it stays unanswered in this book; the ultimate decision going to the population, our future generations, and above all, to you the reader.

BIBLIOGRAPHY

Alfs, Matthew. 1991. *The Evocative Religion of the Jehovah's Witnesses*. Minneapolis: Old Theology Book House.

Avital, Eytan, and Eva Jablonka. 1994. "Social Learning and the Evolution of Behavior." *Animal Behavior* 5. 1195–99.

Axelrod, Robert. 1984. *The Evolution of Cooperation*. New York: Basic Books.

Bonner, John Tyler. 1980. *The Evolution of Culture in Animals*. Princeton: Princeton University Press.

Boyd, Robert, and Peter J. Richerson. 1985. *Culture and the Evolutionary Process*. Chicago: University of Chicago Press.

Brockman, John. Ed. 1990. *Speculations*. New York: Prentice-Hall.

——. 1995. *The Third Culture*. New York: Touchstone.

Brundage, James A. 1987. *Law, Sex, and Christian Society in Medieval Europe*. Chicago: University of Chicago Press.

Brunvand, Jan Harold. 1981. *The Vanishing Hitchhiker*. New York: W. W. Norton.

——. 1984. *The Choking Doberman*. New York: W. W. Norton.

——. 1986. *The Mexican Pet*. New York: W. W. Norton.

——. 1989. *Curses! Broiled Again!* New York: W. W. Norton.

——. 1993. *The Baby Train*. New York: W. W. Norton.

Buss, David M. 1994. *The Evolution of Desire*. New York: Basic Books.

Caldwell, John C., and Pat Caldwell. 1990. "High Fertility in Sub-Saharan Africa." *Scientific American* 262, no. 5. 118–25.

Cloak, F. T. 1975. "Is a Cultural Ethology Possible?" *Human Ecology* 3. 161–82.

Cohen, I. Bernard. 1990. *Benjamin Franklin's Science*. Cambridge: Harvard University Press.

Colford, Paul D. 1993. *The Rush Limbaugh Story: Talent on Loan from God*. New York: St. Martin's Press.

Csikszentmihalyi, Mihaly. 1993. *The Evolving Self*. New York: HarperCollins.

Dawkins, Richard. 1976. *The Selfish Gene*. Oxford: Oxford University Press.

——. 1982. *The Extended Phenotype*. San Francisco: W. H. Freeman.

——. 1986. *The Blind Watchmaker*. New York: W. W. Norton.

————. 1993. "Viruses of the Mind." In *Dennett and His Critics*. Bo Dahlbom. Ed. Cambridge: Blackwell Publishers.

————. 1995. *River out of Eden: A Darwinian View of Life*. New York: Basic Books.

De Alarcon R. 1969. "The Spread of Heroin Abuse in a Community." *Community Health* 1, no. 3. 155–61.

DeLillo, Don. 1991. *Mao II*. New York: Viking Penguin.

Dennett, Daniel C. 1991. *Consciousness Explained*. Boston: Little, Brown.

————. 1995. *Darwin's Dangerous Idea*. New York: Simon & Schuster.

Dessouki, Ali E. Hillal. 1982. *Islamic Resurgence in the Arab World*. New York: Praeger.

Devereux, George. 1976. *A Study of Abortion in Primitive Societies*. New York: International University Press.

de Waal, Frans B. M. 1995. "Bonobo Sex and Society." *Scientific American* 272, no. 3. 82–88.

Diamond, Jared. 1992. *The Third Chimpanzee*. New York: HarperCollins.

Drexler, K. Eric. 1987. *Engines of Creation*. New York: Anchor Press/Doubleday.

Durham, William H. 1991. *Coevolution: Genes, Culture, and Human Diversity*. Stanford: Stanford University Press.

Freud, Sigmund. 1966. *On the History of the Psychoanalytic Movement*. New York: W. W. Norton.

Frisch, Rose E. 1988. "Fatness and Fertility." *Scientific American* 258, no. 3. 88–95.

Fussell, Paul. 1983. *Class*. New York: Ballantine Books.

Gell-Mann, Murray. 1994. *The Quark and the Jaguar: Adventures in the Simple and the Complex*. New York: W. H. Freeman.

Gleick, James. 1987. *Chaos: Making a New Science*. New York: Viking Penguin.

Hammer, Dean H., Hu, Stella, Magnuson, Victoria L., Hu, Nan, and Angela M. L. Pattatucci. 1993. "A Linkage between DNA Markers on the X Chromosome and Male Sexual Orientation." *Science* 261. 321–27.

Hartung, John. 1976. "On Natural Selection and the Inheritance of Wealth." *Current Anthropology* 17. 607–22.

Hofstadter, Douglas R. 1980. *Gödel, Escher, Bach: An Eternal Golden Braid*. New York: Basic Books.

————. 1985. *Metamagical Themas: Questing for the Essence of Mind and Pattern*. New York: Basic Books.

Hofstadter, Douglas R., and Daniel C. Dennett. 1981. *The Mind's I.* New York: Basic Books.

Hostetler, John A. 1993. *Amish Society,* 4th ed. Baltimore: Johns Hopkins University Press.

————. 1974. *Hutterite Society.* Baltimore: Johns Hopkins University Press.

Kashamura, A. 1973. *Famille, sexualité, et couture: Essai sur les mœurs sexuelles et les cultures des peuples des Grand Lacs Africains.* Paris: Payot.

Kuhn, Thomas. 1970. *The Structure of Scientific Revolutions.* Chicago: University of Chicago Press.

Laumann, Edward O., Gagnon, John H., Michael, Robert T., and Stuart Michaels. 1994. *The Social Organization of Sexuality.* Chicago: University of Chicago Press.

Ludlow, Daniel H. Ed. 1992. *Encyclopedia of Mormonism.* New York: Macmillan.

Lumsden, Charles J., and Edward O. Wilson. 1981. *Genes, Mind, and Culture.* Cambridge: Harvard University Press.

Lynch, Aaron. 1991. "Thought Contagion as Abstract Evolution." *Journal of Ideas* 2. 3–10.

Malinowski, Bronislaw. 1932. *The Sexual Life of Savages.* Boston: Beacon Press.

Marty, Martin E., and R. Scott Appleby. Eds. 1991. *Fundamentalism Observed.* Chicago: University of Chicago Press.

Michael, Robert T., Gagnon, John H., Laumann, Edward O., and Gina Kolata. 1994. *Sex in America: A Definitive Survey.* Boston: Little, Brown.

Mirko D. 1990. *History of AIDS.* Princeton: Princeton University Press.

Moritz, Elan. 1990. "Memetic Science. I. General Introduction." *Journal of Ideas* 1. 3–23.

Nowak, Martin, and Karl Sigmund. 1993. "A Strategy of Win–Stay, Lose–Shift That Outperforms Tit-for-Tat in the Prisoner's Dilemma Game." *Nature* 364. 56–58.

Raepke, C. Owen. 1993. *The Evolution of Progress.* New York: Random House.

Ritter, Thomas J. 1992. *Say No to Circumcision.* Aptos: Hourglass Books.

Rogers, Everett M. 1983. *The Diffusion of Innovations.* New York: Free Press.

Rosen, Harold. 1967. *Abortion in America.* Boston: Beacon Press.

Shilts, Randy. 1987. *And the Band Played On: People, Politics, and the AIDS Epidemic.* New York: St. Martin's Press.

Short, R. V. 1984. "Breast Feeding." *Scientific American* 250, no. 4. 35–41.

Stein, Stephen J. 1992. *The Shaker Experience in America.* New Haven: Yale University Press.

Symons, Donald. 1979. *The Evolution of Human Sexuality.* New York: Oxford University Press.

Westoff, Charles F. 1986. "Fertility in the United States." *Science* 234, no. 4776. 554–59.

Witten, Matthew. 1991. "Modeling the Distribution of a 'Meme' in a Simple Age Distribution Population. I. A Kinetics Approach and Some Alternative Models." *Journal of Ideas* 2. 19–25.

Wright, Robert. 1994. *The Moral Animal.* New York: Pantheon.

INDEX

Abortion
  Catholic beliefs, 168
  controversy over, 163–68
Abortion memes
  murderous abortion, 166–67
  pro- and antiabortion, 164–65, 167
  prochoice and prolife, 166–68
Abortion rights meme, 164, 166
Adultery, 103
AIDS virus
  conditions for infection, 136
  effect on promiscuity, 78
  genetic adaptation, 142. *See also* HIV
Altruism, 109
Amish Society (Hostetler), 1–2
Ancestor worship, 97–98
Anthropology
  memetic, 26–27
Anthropology
  cultural, 24–27
Apocalypse meme, 110
Approach-role memes, 84
Astrology, 140–41
Avital, Eytan, 5
Axelrod, Robert, 31, 109

Barriers
  language, 168–69
  to thought contagion, 12–16
  to transmission of beliefs, 12–16
Belief propagation
  explored by memetics, 22
Beliefs
  breast-feeding, 137–38
  in Christian apocalypse and rapture, 109–10
  circumcision, 136–37
  health-related, 135–55
  immunized against proselytism, 6, 109–10
  in marriage, 48
  mass, 13
  memetic explanations, 12, 37–38
  recombination of, 11–12
  sexually transmitted disease, 78, 145
  treatment in cultural anthropology, 24–27
  triggering proselytizing, 5–6
Belief transmission
  barriers to, 12–16
  marriage, 48
Biological factors
  affecting sexual preference, 79
  parental love for children, 43
Biparentalism, monogamous, 44–47
Birth control
  acceptance of, 92
  through interrupted intercourse, 91

DATE DUE

HIGHSMITH #45115